EULA MAE BAUGH

LESSONS FOR LIVING

*From 60 Years of
Faithful Bible Teaching*

Edited by Bo Prosser
Foreword by Daniel Vestal

© 2018
Published in the United States by Nurturing Faith Inc., Macon GA,
www.nurturingfaith.net.

Library of Congress Cataloging-in-Publication Data is available.

ISBN 978-1-63528-044-9

All rights reserved. Printed in the United States of America

"I did not have the pleasure of attending a Sunday School class taught by Eula Mae Baugh, but I did enjoy many pleasurable and meaningful meetings with her. Eula Mae was an outstanding, strong lady with many talents. She and her husband worked with other people and organizations that have made this world richer in many ways. They were generous with financial gifts and made God's world a better place in which to live by personally working with other. I treasure my memories of this wonderful lady."

—*Mrs. Herb (Joy) Reynolds*
Waco, Texas

"Mrs. Baugh, one of the best Bible teachers I ever had, was always prepared to deliver clear biblical truths and provide useful applications for living an exemplary life. Her biblical teaching skills were honed, no doubt, by her being reared in a Baptist preacher's home. She was so dedicated, and always gracious, loving, caring, and generous with her time. Mrs. Baugh's Christian walk—her compassion for family, friends, and others—was obvious in every aspect and activity of her life."

—*Jack D. Carlson*
Houston, Texas

"It is with great fondness that I remember my special friend, Eula Mae Baugh, a wonderful Christian, Bible teacher, and Southern lady. I never had a Sunday School teacher more knowledgeable of the Bible than Mrs. Baugh. She spent many hours each week researching and studying for our singles class that she taught in a down-to-earth manner for everyone to understand. Mrs. Baugh, an inspiration, was always gracious, compassionate and a true friend."

—*Jane Bugg*
Meadowlakes, Texas

"Mrs. Baugh was such a special lady. She was a wonderful Bible teacher who kept her class interested and involved. I always enjoyed the small get-togethers in her home. We had great fun talking and also eating the delicious dinners she prepared. She was one of a kind and is missed to this day."

—*Lynda Spinks*
Garden Oaks, Texas

"I have heard it said by a master teacher that when a teacher loves her subject matter and loves her students, miracles happen. As a lifelong teacher of Bible studies, I was mesmerized and inspired by the lessons included in this book about the life of Eula Mae Baugh.

"It was the consistency in communicating the biblical material and applying the lesson to the everyday lives of her students that impressed me most, and while she was a woman of her era, the life lessons she taught are applicable for today. Her method of involving the class in the process reminds me of Jesus the Teacher who taught not only by what he said or did, but by his very character.

"Eula Mae Baugh—beautiful, dignified, gracious, and strong—clearly revealed a love for her subject matter and her students, and my guess is that by her transparency, her generosity, her practicality and her involvement with her class members, she changed their lives.

"I feel her strength and *joie de vivre* lived out in her daughter Babs and her granddaughters, Julie and Jackie. Clearly, she taught them well. She teaches us well, even now, through this book. We do well to learn from her."

—*Jeanie Miley*
Spiritual director, speaker, retreat leader,
and author of 13 books

"Seldom have the laity received the appreciation and recognition they should. In Baptist life, they are the soul of the church. Thank goodness for this look at the life of one such laywoman, an intimate and inspiring look that should cause each of us to ask, 'What am I called to be and do as a part of Christ's church—and how can I love as he has loved me?' I think Eula Mae would agree that we are not called to do nothing. She was called to teach Sunday School, but the result of answering her call was that she laughingly and lovingly helped those who heard her voice have a more vital relationship to Christ and his community.

"*Lessons for Living* brings Eula Mae alive to a new generation and those beyond her family so that we, too, can hear her voice. At the very least, it could enhance the teaching of many faithful Sunday School teachers who are always looking for ways to improve and have the kind of impact that Eula Mae did."

—*Connie McNeill*
Associate Pastor for Administration and Discipleship
Second Baptist Church, Liberty, Mo.

"Eula Mae Baugh was an extraordinary Baptist leader who left a long-lasting legacy of generosity to Baptist mission work and institutions in Texas and around the world. Thanks to Bo Prosser for giving us a window into the teaching ministry of Eula Mae through a sampling of about 60 years of Sunday School lessons. These lessons reveal a Baptist woman who was indeed called to ministry, traditional in some respects but also innovative and inspiring. This volume reminds readers of the importance of lay-led ministry and how that faithfulness looks from the pew. As a lay leader, committed church member, Sunday School teacher and philanthropist, the contributions of Eula Mae Baugh to our Baptist family are enduring and overflowing."

—*Aaron Weaver*
Communications Director
Cooperative Baptist Fellowship

"In strictest theological terms, this book is known as 'a double whammy.' First, it's a stellar tribute to one of the finest Baptist Christians who graced this earth, Eula Mae Baugh. We see her as an exemplary Bible study teacher, but also as a loving wife, mother and grandmother, as well as a devoted community leader, church member, businesswoman, and philanthropist. In these pages we learn about her and learn from her. Second, it's a stunning collection of Bible lessons. Eula Mae taught Scripture as a practical guide to a faithful, fulfilling life. With only the slightest tweaks, these lessons are as relevant today as they were the Sunday she taught them—and far better than most of us are likely to prepare."

—*Marv Knox*
Field Coordinator
CBF Southwest

"I opened *Lessons for Living* like a time capsule, curious to see what it held from the life and teachings of Eula Mae Baugh. In it I found timeless resources for teaching from the Bible. Even more, it gave me a chance to peer into the heart and life of an accomplished woman. Here are the writings of a deepened faith. They bear testimony to a soul that trusted God along the marvelous adventures of her days. . . . Here are windows not only to the grounded soul of a Baptist leader, but also to a dedicated servant who worked at her teaching responsibility. . . . I feel as though I have been given a glimpse into Eula Mae's spirit, faith, and dedication through her teachings."

—*Charles Qualls*
Pastor
Franklin (Va.) Baptist Church

"Eula Mae was witty and wise, with a touch of spiritual sassiness. She was fun and funny—all of which comes through in this collection of her writings. She honored God with her life and by teaching Sunday School. If you want a fresh read on how to teach the Scriptures, open her book. The pages will turn themselves."

—*Les Hollon*
Pastor
Trinity Baptist Church
San Antonio, Texas

"The life of Eula Mae Baugh is a testament to what God can do with one faithful person committed to live out her Christian call through years of weekly devotion to deep Bible study and to teaching adult Sunday School. Eula Mae exemplified those lessons in her love for family, for friends, and for those in need and as she helped grow a community of faith. Today we are fortunate to have access to Eula Mae's 'lessons for living' that can be used for individual devotion or small group discussion."

—*Vicki Hollon*
Minister to Adults
Trinity Baptist Church
San Antonio, Texas

"Where would Cooperative Baptists be without the Baugh family? There is no doubt that their faithful generosity is forming our fellowship and investing in our collaborative future. This book offers the reader a glimpse back in time to where it all began: the Sunday School classroom of Mrs. Eula Mae Baugh. Through her wit and wisdom, Eula Mae creatively challenged her family and friends to grow deeper in faith. Her lessons are practical and timeless, and this book has the potential to inspire a new generation of Christians."

—*Rob Fox*
President-elect
CBF Church Benefits

Contents

Beginning at the End 1
An Introduction to Eula Mae Baugh

Eula Mae Baugh 3
Obituary

My Mother... 5
A Tribute by Babs Baugh

A Life of Love and Devotion... 7
Foreword by Daniel Vestal

Growing in Belief, Community, and Servanthood..................... 11
Eula Mae Baugh's Teaching Approach

Observations and Opportunities 15
*Lessons for Living from Eula Mae Baugh

Thoughts on Faith and Life 123
The Wit and Wisdom of Eula Mae Baugh

Our Grandmother 131
A Tribute by Jackie Baugh Moore and Julie Baugh Cloud

* See page viii for a topical and biblically referenced list of the 53 "Lessons for Living."

Patriarchal Narratives
16 Abraham and Sarah (Gen. 17)
18 Abraham and Isaac (Gen. 22)
20 The heritage of Isaac (Gen. 24, 25:5-6)
22 Jacob and Esau (Gen. 27, 28)
24 Jacob and Laban (Gen. 31)
26 Joseph and his brothers (Gen. 42–45)

Ten Commandments
28 Balancing obedience and relationships (Exod. 20:1-20)
30 I am the Lord your God (Exod. 20:2-6)
32 Do not take the name of the Lord in vain (Exod. (20:8)
34 Remember the Sabbath (Exod. 20:8-11)
36 You shall not covet (Exod. 20:17)

Book of Psalms
38 Stand tall and look good (Ps. 1)
40 Sing! (Ps. 8)
42 A psalm of prayers (Ps. 119)
44 Intimacy with God (Ps. 139)

Old Testament
46 Spying on the promised land (Num. 13–14)
48 Becoming the people of God (Deut. 27–29)
50 A good woman (Prov. 31)
52 Citizens of two nations (Amos 4, 5)

Christmas
54 The gift of faithfulness (Matt. 1)
56 The gift of availability (Luke 2)
58 The gifts of the wise men (Matt. 2:1-12)

Sermon on the Mount
60 Happy Christians (Matt. 5:1-15)
62 Keeping the law (Matt. 5:27-37)
64 Prayer and priorities (Matt. 6:1-18)
66 Don't worry about worry! (Matt. 6:24-34)
68 The golden rule (Matt. 7:1-12)

Book of Matthew
70 The demands of relationships (Matt. 10:21-35)
72 Forgiveness without limits (Matt. 18:21-35)
74 The things to come (Matt. 24)

Holy Week
76 In remembrance (Matt. 26:1-56)
78 Betrayal (Matt. 26:57-67, 27:1-26)

Book of John
80 A new life for Nicodemus (John 3:1-16)
82 Sight vs. seeing (John 9:1-12)
84 Blindness (John 9:13-41)
86 Freedom from fear and grief (John 11, 17:3)

Paul's Writings
88 Pentecost (Acts 2)
90 Preaching in Rome (Acts 28:11-30)
92 Do all things work together for good? (Rom. 8:28)
94 The superiority of love (1 Cor. 13:1-7)
96 Living fully into our calling (Eph. 1)
98 Shining stars (Phil. 2:12-30)
100 The art of living (Phil. 4)
102 No fear! (2 Tim. 1:7)
104 Inspiration of the Bible (2 Tim. 5:16)

New Testament
106 The call of God (Mark 1:16–2:17)
108 The mystery of mysteries (Rev. 1)

Stewardship
110 The call to give (2 Cor.8:1-15)
112 The focus of giving (Mal. 2:17–3:12)
114 The miracle of giving (Exod. 35–40)
116 The accountability of giving (Matt. 25:14-30)

Baptist Principles
118 Baptist by choice
120 Sharing and observing

Dedicated to:

Gail, Jamie, and Katie for making me a better man

Sarah, Lois, and all the wonderful women who have formed me as a minister and leader

And especially to Eula Mae for living out her calling and giving us all such a deep Baptist legacy

Beginning at the End

An Introduction to Eula Mae Baugh

This book begins at the end! The idea for the book came from a conversation between Daniel Vestal and Babs Baugh concerning the life and work of Babs' mom, Eula Mae Baugh. Daniel called me and gave me the honor of trying to piece together more than 60 years of Sunday School lessons, sharing her wit and wisdom, and giving the reader glimpses of an extraordinary woman.

I want you to see her obituary before you dive into the rest of the book. She was a woman ahead of her time—way ahead! And, she was also a woman of her time. At many places in the book she speaks from her place in time.

In her Sunday School lessons she usually used the male language for God—for which she was unapologetic—and also quoted from the King James Version. After all, she was a product of her culture and her upbringing. She was raised by a Baptist preacher who, in the best sense of parenting, taught her the basics as he knew it.

My editor and I intentionally tried not to modernize her words. We've left her language alone for the most part because it represents her traditional understandings of God. Remember, these lesson plans came from the 1950s and 60s. She never expected that her notes would be published, much less put into book form. If she had, I am certain that she would have challenged the purely masculine nouns and pronouns around the name of Jehovah God in today's context.

Yet, in her upbringing Eula Mae was also given the freedom to grow and be herself. In her lessons you'll see her as strong-minded and independent, brave and courageous, tender and loving. You'll see glimpses into her teaching (and preaching), and you'll see her challenging her students to think for themselves.

These are amazing pages. I am honored to have been a part of this project. I'm grateful to Daniel Vestal and the Baugh Family for the opportunity to sort through Eula Mae's personal files. I'm appreciative of John Pierce and Nurturing Faith Publishing for their energy and grace in helping us get this to print. Clarissa Strickland served as my personal editor and made these pages much more alive than they could have been. And, Libby Allen of the Baugh Center kept Daniel and me on pace! I'm also grateful to my wife, Gail, who graciously gave me the time to hide away, research and write.

Most of all, I'm especially thankful to Eula Mae. I'm grateful for her leadership and commitment to the church and more for her commitment to Jesus the Christ. Her files have been fascinating. Her words are as alive today as they were when she put the lesson plans together. And her spirit continues to swirl around all of us. We are richer for the contributions she made to God's world—and that she continues to make.

And so, we begin at the end. . . Or, is this just the next beginning?

Bo Prosser

Eula Mae Baugh
Obituary

Eula Mae Tharp Baugh went to be with her Savior on the 29th of August 2007. She was a creative and compassionate woman and she will be dearly missed by her family and friends. Eula Mae was born in 1918 in Anna, Illinois to Rev. Ralph H. Tharp and Clara Hinson Tharp. Although her mother died when Eula Mae was two, she was blessed when her father married Edna Jane Glasscock who became her mother and truly shaped her life. Eula Mae was the oldest of five children. A beauty inside and out, Eula Mae met her loving husband while attending the University of Houston night school. They were an amazing team with an incredible love story that lasted for the 71 years of their marriage. As a team, they created a small frozen food company in the back bedroom of their home. Eula Mae took phone orders, did bookkeeping, and cared for their home and daughter while Johnny made deliveries and sales calls. When the little company grew, and a vision for a bigger company became reality, Eula Mae suggested the name Sysco Foods. Today, Sysco is the largest company of its kind in the world. The other owners of the original companies that became the Sysco Corporation were brave, visionary, honest people that were life-long friends to the entire Baugh family. Growing up as the child of a Baptist preacher, Eula Mae was mission minded from her earliest days. She spent her life serving others. She and Johnny helped churches around the world including places like Brazil, Europe and Africa and all over Texas. Because of her influence and generosity, buildings at Baptist Child and Family Services in San Antonio, Houston Baptist University, and Memorial-Hermann Hospital honor her name. The campuses at George W. Truett Theological Seminary at Baylor University and the new campus at the Baptist University of the Americas also carry the Baugh name. One of Eula Mae's most significant accomplishments was her special gift for teaching Sunday School. She began teaching as a teenager and taught for more than 60 years. Her research and methods of teaching were legendary.

Her classes were fascinating as she studied 25 hours per week in order to thoroughly fulfill her calling. A spirit of adventure led Eula Mae to plan many travel excursions for her family. She and Johnny traveled all over the world from the North to the South Poles. She introduced a love of travel and learning about other cultures to her family. Their travel involved business, pleasure and mission work. Eula Mae has received some of the highest honors bestowed by Baylor University. She and Johnny were instrumental in creating Truett Seminary at Baylor. They were involved in many other philanthropic causes including Central Baptist Theological Seminary, Baptist University of the Americas, Mary Hardin Baylor University, Houston Baptist University, Baptist Child and Family Services, the *Baptist Standard*, the Associated Baptist Press, the Baptist Joint Committee and numerous works through the Baptist General Convention of Texas. Eula Mae and Johnny have one daughter, Barbara Nell (Babs) Baugh and two granddaughters, Jackie and Julie. Eula Mae made it her life's mission to provide love, laughter, music, fun, adventure, security and gentle Christian guidance to her three girls and her husband. She personified the qualities listed in the 31st chapter of Proverbs. Never could a life be lived more fully, more gracefully or more compassionately. Eula Mae lived her life as a servant to her God, her family, her friends and any person who needed her. A team to the last day on earth, her adoring husband John F. Baugh preceded her to the Father by 25 weeks. Eula Mae is survived by her daughter, Babs Baugh, and husband John Jarrett of San Antonio; her granddaughters Jackie Moore and husband Kim Moore of San Antonio and Julie Ortiz and husband Carlos Ortiz of Austin; her great grandchildren Sterling, Katie and Jake Moore and Breck and Alexa Mae Ortiz; sisters Evelyn Simons, Jo House, Charlotte Smith and brother Warren Tharp and many nieces and nephews and cherished friends. Friends are cordially invited to a visitation with the family from nine until eleven o'clock in the morning on Saturday, the 1st of September, at Geo. H. Lewis & Sons, 1010 Bering Drive. A funeral service will be conducted at two o'clock in the afternoon on Saturday, the 1st of September in the sanctuary of Tallowood Baptist Church, 555 Tallowood Drive in Houston, with the Rev. Dr. Duane Brooks and Rev. Dr. Daniel Vestal officiating. An orchestral prelude will begin fifteen minutes prior to two o'clock. Interment will follow, via an escorted cortege, at Forest Park Westheimer Cemetery, 12800 Westheimer Road in Houston.

Copied from *Houston Express-News*
Sept. 1, 2007

My Mother

A Tribute by Babs Baugh

My mother "never not" taught Sunday School. I know that's bad grammar, but it's simply a fact that Eula Mae Baugh taught the Bible to people most of her life, and she did it with a flair and flourish that was uniquely her own. She started teaching children as a teenager and continued by teaching college students, single adults, married adults, and finally senior adults.

Mama, as I affectionately called her, was the eldest of six children. Her father, Rev. Ralph Tharp, was a pastor/church planter who would stay at a church until it was self-sufficient and then move to another place. That explains why each of the six children was born in a different state. After high school Mama enrolled in night school at the University of Houston, where she met the man God had created for her, John Baugh.

At age 18 she and John were married in her family home, spent their honeymoon at his parents' home in Waco, and then began saving to buy their own home from their $7.00-a-week salary. John worked for A&P Food Stores, and Mama took a job in a doctor's office. Something else important happened. They joined Second Baptist Church in Houston, where Mama began teaching Sunday School. Papo, as I affectionately called my father, was the superintendent of the Sunday School department and Mama was the Bible teacher. From the very beginning they were a team.

Mama felt as called to be a Sunday School teacher as preachers feel called to preach. She purchased concordances and commentaries that were recommended by pastors she respected and trusted. She spent about 25 hours a week studying for each lesson. If her interpretation differed from that of the commentaries, she would seek advice from other Bible students. And, she prayed a lot.

Mama was dedicated to applying the words of the Bible to situations that would be helpful in the everyday lives of her students. She was a life-long learner and was always seeking to improve in her academic and spiritual understanding of Scripture. She was always looking for ways to enhance her teaching. For example, when it was time for the Jewish Passover, she would seek advice from a rabbi friend and then offer the complete Passover meal to her class.

But her teaching on Sundays was accompanied by her love and care for class members during the week. She hosted parties on holidays, sightseeing boat rides on the Houston ship channel, and visits on the weekend to the family ranch—which included five meals. She was always planning games, trips, and events that celebrated birthdays and anniversaries. And in times of sorrow, loss or disappointment, Mama was right there with class members to talk and listen. She sent postcards and made phone calls and visits. Her real accomplishment was making her students feel like someone cared, which she did. Her classes were heavily involved in funding mission projects and missionaries. Our family lovingly labeled her "Dottie Do Good," and Papo ordered her special license plates that had one word on them: "Whizzo."

Eula Mae and John Baugh's partnership in their church extended into all of their life. Early in their marriage Papo decided it was time for them to try and start a business. He reasoned that his young age would allow him to get a job if the business didn't work out.

Frozen foods were just being introduced to the world, so that was his choice of products. He would make sales call in the mornings and deliveries in the afternoon, while Mama stayed home to keep the accounting books, answer telephone calls, pay the bills, send invoices, and take orders. She did all this while taking care of me.

On Saturdays Mama would take me either to shop or ride the bus downtown to the city library. On Sundays we all attended Sunday School and church and then went home for lunch (which was usually pot roast), after which we would go to the office with a quilt where Mama and I would take a nap while Papo worked. We returned to the church for evening service. For some this seems like a dull existence, but Mama made it fun.

Eula Mae and John Baugh traveled the world together and built a food business that is the largest wholesale distributer in the country (SYSCO) with a net income of $949 million and that employs 65,000 people. Mama got to ring the opening bell at the New York Exchange. But she would say that teaching Sunday School was one of the greatest joys of her life.

A Life of Love and Devotion*
A Foreword by Daniel Vestal

The Sunday before Eula Mae Baugh died, there was a review by Darcy Steinke in the *New York Times* book review section of Mary Gordon's book, *Circling My Mother*. Here's a quote from that review in the August 26, 2007 issue:

> These days, we seem to have two kinds of religious books. Those like *The Purpose-Driven Life*, the pastor Rick Warren's self-help book, insipidly set out conservative precepts, encouraging us to join churches, obey their doctrines and center our spiritual lives around them, no matter how limiting those lives might be in that context alone. At the other end of the spectrum are gleeful repudiations of religion like Christopher Hitchen's atheist manifesto, *God Is Not Great*. But Hitchen's definition of religion is childlike and reductive; he completely discounts the longing many of us feel for divinity.

Steinke went on to say that what is needed in today's world are books and people who don't pontificate about their faith, but who attend to their own religious life and vocation with a full belief in the love of God. This is what Eula Mae Baugh did. She lived as a woman, as a wife, as a mother, as a friend, as a church member, as a student and teacher of the Bible, as a Christian, and as a person—full of love and devotion. While the lessons included in this book are only a part of her legacy, they do reflect an amazing life of religious vocation.

There was a matriarchal quality to Eula Mae Baugh, and not just because she was married to a patriarchal figure for 60 years. She was, in her own right, a towering figure. In the words of Proverbs 31, she was "a woman who feared the Lord . . . was clothed with strength and dignity . . . a wife of noble character . . . whose children arise to call her blessed."

I confess that the first few times I met Eula Mae I was somewhat intimidated—even more so than by her husband. Somehow John Baugh and I had a chemistry of friendship that resulted in an almost immediate bonding. But with Eula Mae, it was different. She had an almost regal bearing about her. She was striking in appearance and demeanor, and one need be around her for only a short time to realize that she was clever, witty, and discerning.

It didn't take long before my intimidation turned to great affection and deep appreciation. I soon came to know her as a delightful and engaging friend who enjoyed conversation, good food, music, and laughter. And she especially enjoyed sharing all of these with other people. She had a twinkle in her eyes and a spring in her step, especially when she was doing something for someone else.

Eula Mae offered her friendship to so many people and to so many different kinds of people. It was her love and devotion that stood out through the years as a defining character quality. She was something of a model, an example, an encouragement to all of us in how we should live.

*Adaptation of the message delivered on September 1, 2007, at Tallowood Baptist Church in Houston, Texas, at "An Hour of Worship, Remembrance and Celebration," a service of worship honoring the life and passing of Eula Mae Baugh.

Dr. Herb Reynolds was president of Baylor University for many years. He and his wife, Joy, were long-time friends of the Baughs. Seldom did Dr. Reynolds use humor, but I can remember a story he told about himself when he and Joy were dating. It seems he told a pastor that they were having their "devotions" together. And then with a slight smile, he said, "I was devoted to her and she was devoted to me."

How else can one describe the marriage of John and Eula Mae Baugh except to say they were "devoted" to each other? And how else can one describe the relationship Eula Mae had with her daughter, Babs, and her two granddaughters, Jackie and Julie, except to say that they were devoted to each other. It was a love and devotion that bonded them into a remarkable family.

Eula Mae was also devoted to Scripture. She loved to study the Bible, and she loved to teach the Bible. The first time I saw the voluminous material she had gathered and produced for her Sunday School class I was overwhelmed. It rivaled the material of many experienced pastors. She had a diligence and dedication to learn the Scriptures and to help others learn the Scriptures. This book, if nothing else, is a tribute to a woman who gave her life to Bible learning and Bible teaching.

Eula Mae was also devoted to the Body of Christ. Although she had reason to be cynical about the church, she never was. Unlike some "preachers' kids" and other life-long church members who are immersed in congregational and denominational politics, she never flagged in her devotion to the church of Jesus Christ.

And then, Eula Mae loved her friends. In small and large ways she demonstrated an unflagging devotion to people. She was not only like Mary, who sat at the feet of Jesus listening and learning, but she also was like Martha, who offered gracious hospitality. Like Lydia, she opened her heart and her home to others. Like Dorcas, she was "always doing good and helping the poor." And like Phoebe, she was a servant of the Lord, although she never held the title of "deacon."

But most of all, Eula Mae was devoted to the Lord in a very loving and Christ-like relationship. This, to me, is the *summon bonum*, the greatest good of the Christian experience. It is the "pearl of great price," "the holy grail," the one virtue that is to be prized above all others. God, who loves us passionately and is devoted to us, wants our love and devotion in return. And God wants us to love one another. This is not only the great commandment but also the new commandment that Jesus Christ embodied.

The cover article of *Time* magazine the week before Eula Mae died was about Mother Teresa, that icon of 20th century Christianity. The article chronicled the struggle, darkness, and spiritual absence she felt for much of her public ministry. Yet, despite her inner pain, she never faltered in her self-emptying love for God and for people, especially the poor. The article in the August 23, 2007 issue concludes with these words:

> The tendency in our spiritual life but also in our more general attitude toward love is that our feelings are all that is going on.... And to us the totality of love is what we feel. But to really love someone requires commitment, fidelity, and vulnerability. Mother Teresa wasn't feeling Christ's love, and she could have shut down. But she was up at 4:30 every morning for Jesus, and still writing to him. "Your happiness is all I want." That is a powerful example even if you are not talking in religious terms.

Love and devotion are not just about feelings or about words, either said or sung. Love and devotion are not just about performing religious rituals or ceremonies but about works of justice, deeds of mercy, acts of kindness, service, and sacrifice. This is the life of love and devotion that Eula Mae Baugh lived.

Like so many women before and after her, who are little-known or recognized, her contribution to the Kingdom of God is immeasurable. Thankfully, this book is a reminder of her contribution and theirs too.

(Daniel Vestal is Distinguished University Professor of Baptist Leadership and Director of the Eula Mae and John Baugh Center for Baptist Leadership at Mercer University.)

Growing in Belief, Community, and Servanthood
Eula Mae Baugh's Teaching Approach

I did not know Eula Mae Baugh. I never had the pleasure of meeting her or John. Over these past months of research, however, I feel as though I've come to know her. She was a confident Baptist lay woman who was well ahead of her time. Her lesson outlines indicate that she taught in such a manner as to engage her classes. She was self-assured and didn't mind challenging her class participants. She was fun-loving and looked for ways to inject humor into her teaching. She was aware of her times, ready to speak to the issues of her day. And she wasn't just teaching; she was calling her class members to action.

Eula Mae was not content to follow the typical teaching approaches of her day. In the 1950s and 60s, teaching methods were simpler. People were committed to Sunday School for information, inspiration, and fellowship. The class was built around the thinking of, "You sit still while I instill what I have distilled through my study this week."

Eula Mae would have no part of that approach. She was always prepared, for sure. She had moments of lecture to bring central points to the teaching event. But she also made sure that her class bonded, talked together, and laughed with each other. And, as class participants exited the classroom, she expected them to put their faith into practice, applying the principles that had been discussed.

The ability to teach people biblical truths is one of the most challenging aspects of spiritual discipleship. Teaching is crucial to helping others grow and mature as followers of Christ. Eula Mae knew that she was "called" to be a teacher; to present challenges, information, and inspiration week after week. After delving deeply into her teaching plans, I can tell you that she was always prepared, that she cared for her class members, that she loved her church, and that she never tried to "bluff" her way through a lesson.

She took her calling as a teacher seriously. In one lesson plan there was a handwritten note in the margin that read, "I know that there are some of you who wish I would quit teaching this class. . . ." While she didn't finish that thought, I'm pretty sure she might have said, ". . . and when God tells me I'm done, then I'll quit!" She was deeply committed. And she was more than just the typical "homemaker" of the 50s and 60s. She was active in the church, for sure. She was also active in the community, leading in other areas of development efforts. And, she was deeply committed to her husband, John, helping him as he built a successful national corporation.

Because many of Eula Mae's lesson outlines were written on the backs of old calendars, I was fortunate enough to get an idea of just how busy she was with helping John, doing her community activities and, of course, following her beloved Houston Astros. And in all that, she was in class every week, prepared and ready to lead.

She collected ideas from everywhere—newspapers, magazines, church bulletins, real life experiences. I was given two huge file boxes of anecdotes that she had collected *and* filed away by subject for use in her lessons. She gave credit to her sources where possible, and I have done the same. There are also anecdotes that may be included whose citations have been lost or are untraceable. Our apologies to any contributors that may not be cited.

Eula Mae Baugh knew how to teach! She was equipped with effective teaching methods and resources. She modeled for her class effective outreach and ministry methods. She shared leadership by growing "assistant teachers" and small group leaders who would go on to teach other classes. She blended traditional teaching methods with innovative approaches so that her classes were engaging, fun, inspirational, and relational. She understood that involvement, especially in the large classes she led, would be very important. Here is an excerpt from a note to her assistant teachers:

Dear Teaching Assistants:

The main purpose of having "huddle and hassle" groups is to lead EACH person to get involved. They might not talk out loud, but at least we will get them to begin thinking about the subject.

It is not as important that we get a good report from your group as it is that they participate. So please do not lecture. Just try to bring them out. You will not have time for everyone to speak, but they should feel good about sharing.

You will only have six to eight minutes for discovery. Time will be limited. You'll also only have three to four minutes for reporting.

Here's the format we will use:

1. Ask them to read the assigned scripture silently. It won't take long.

2. Ask pertinent questions which can bring out truths. You can make up your own questions or use the ones provided.

3. If necessary, take notes from the discussion so you can summarize to the rest of us. Better yet, ask someone in your group to make the summary presentation.

4. If you have difficulty getting them started, you might want to share a comment or two of your own.

Good luck and thanks!

As a teacher of adults, Eula Mae was able to communicate effectively on a consistent basis. My own ministry mission statement has always been: "People go where they know they've been prepared for and are cared for." She certainly embodied that statement. She guided the class session with confidence and was open to class discussions. Class members knew they were prepared for and cared for. She had large classes, with 50 or more present each week.

She also knew how to use humor and support materials. Sometimes her handouts were handcut and handwritten, not professionally published but nevertheless effective and thought-provoking. One handout was a cutout heart with typed references to stewardship copied on the inside. On one handout, titled "Purely Personal Poop," she asked lighthearted fill-in-the-blank questions such as: What's your favorite food and television show, a secret ambition, and a pet peeve? These were fun, noncontroversial questions that allowed the class to have a good time while learning a thing or two about each other.

Eula Mae knew how to care for her class. Often she wrote notes in the margins of her lesson outlines to mention certain class members and their accomplishments or to remind herself to send a card to someone or to visit in a home or hospital. In one class about the genealogy of Jesus she compared the biblical family to her Sunday School family and their special gifts and contributions to the church and the community.

There is no doubt that she celebrated with her class members, cried with them when they hurt, and was present with them for important times. "Prepared for and cared for" doesn't happen automatically. We have to be intentional in preparation and care. Being intentional is scheduling and protecting times for ministry and study. There is no doubt that she did all this and more.

I found this handwritten note attached to one of Eula Mae's teaching plans. I've included it because I think it shows the heart of this woman in caring for those around her:

Dear Alex,

In these days of tender memories and difficult adjustment, may I share with you a simple verse that was shared to us when we lost our only son? People's support meant so much to us.

We know from experience that Heaven will be nearer from now on because part of you is already there. And, Easter will take on new meaning each year.

Our love and prayers accompany you. Grief is the price we pay for love. If given the choice, we would not have foregone the love in order to avoid the grief.

Much love,
Eula Mae and John

GOALS

The outcomes of Eula Mae's teaching were testimony to her effectiveness. She challenged her classes to grow in personal faith, in community, and in church attendance and influence. She challenged them to grow more deeply in spirituality and discipleship. Consistently encountering biblical truth leads us to closeness with God and with one another. Eula Mae would not settle for her class to just sit and listen. She expected them to be better prepared to be servants in the Kingdom of God. She was never shy about challenging her classes to tithe or to give more or to share Jesus with everyone—from friends at work to the cashier at the supermarket.

She also challenged her class to share thoughts about lesson ideas in order to deepen their intimacy with one another. There is no way to sit in a Sunday School class week after week and not grow friendships! She understood this and challenged her class members to reach out to others, both inside the church and outside the church. She wanted them to help make the world a better place; to engage social issues, political issues, business issues, Kingdom-of-God issues. And she wanted them to do these together in ministry, discipleship, and evangelism.

This lady was also not afraid to tackle the tough issues of her day. She knew that race relations, labor relations, and foreign relations were challenges for our country. She knew that marriage and family stresses must be dealt with. She taught with unabashed confidence that the church was the one hope for the world. She told her class members that if they were growing in belief, community and servanthood, the message of their "great" class would spread—because most people want to be around good things that are happening.

Eula Mae consistently taught about bringing others to church, telling others about Jesus, the importance of tithing, and how that faith and works go together. She wanted her class and her church to lead others to Christ and to have Christian principles that affect business, industry, politics, and relationships. She knew that in order to have the confidence and the information to do such, one had to be in church. On several occasions from her teaching notes she would gently admonish her classes that they had to be present at church to be the growing disciples that God expected them to be.

APPLICATIONS
The outline template and the ideas in each of the following lessons belong to Eula Mae Baugh. Because she didn't write out manuscripts, however, I had to complete some of her reflections. I tried prayerfully and carefully to represent the spirit of this amazing woman. This has been a spiritual journey for me. At times I felt sure that the Holy Spirit was translating the spirit of Eula Mae Baugh through me.

The lessons in the next section can be used as small group discussions. A leader can use them to guide discussions related to issues highlighted at the time of their writing, some of which are just as challenging today. The lessons can also be used as individual devotions. You may find yourself spending hours with these lessons, wrestling with yourself and your spirit. If you use this for personal devotion, let me suggest that you record ideas that emerge, as in journaling, or write prayers.

However you choose to use these lessons, don't ignore the words of the writer. Eula Mae was a force to be reckoned with. She was a Baptist lay leader, but above all she was a disciple of Christ—a generous giver of her talents, time, and resources to her church and to many more Christian and world-changing causes.

There is much for us to learn from Eula Mae Baugh. She might be considered a "saint" in the Baptist world if indeed we had saints, although she would have been too humble to accept such a title. I think she would be most pleased to be remembered as a committed disciple of Christ who did her best to help make the world a better place for ALL!

Observations and Opportunities
Lessons for Living from Eula Mae Baugh

Abraham and Sarah
Genesis 17

OPENING

There is a time to laugh, according to the writer of Ecclesiastes. What makes us laugh? What we laugh at often reveals a great deal about our attitudes in life!

In today's lesson Abraham and Sarah laugh out loud. This is not a polite smile or a short little "tee hee" snicker. This is the deep belly laugh that brings tears to one's eyes. Abraham and Sarah hear news from God that can be met with only this kind of laughter.

Abraham has become disgusted with the idolatry of his people. He is sincerely searching for God. Abraham needs to get his head together; he wants to bring about change. And so he is searching for God. Faith that is willing to risk all to venture out for God will certainly be rewarded.

If we can see every step of the way, do we really have faith? Abraham can't see his way, but he takes the risk to look for God. And when we sincerely seek, we always find! So when God calls him, Abraham is ready.

OBSERVATIONS ON THE TEXT

As Abraham searches and ponders, he faces many dangers. As God calls, he also reassures us: "I will be your shield. I will be your protection." When we are about the will of our Lord, there will certainly be dangers. And when we are about the will of our Lord, he promises us and reassures us, "I will be your shield and protection too!" God offers us purpose and, as we respond faithfully, God offers his promise and his protection.

God promises more than protection and presence. God says to Abraham, "If you will be blameless before me, I will make from you a great nation." This is more than a promise; it is a covenant. A covenant is a solemn agreement between two or more persons or groups to do or not do a certain thing. This covenant represents a deep relationship between God and Abraham. But the covenant does not materialize immediately. Like the rest of us, Abraham has to wait a while for God to act.

God never works on our timetable. We are all tested as to the patience and consistency of our faith. As a righteous man, Abraham will be tested many times. We face the same challenges. We often pray to God and expect immediate responses. Waiting is the hard part. But God will not be made to jump through hoops on our behalf. We are the ones who must stay faithful, who must not give up, but wait patiently and hopefully for God's promises to be fulfilled. And, God always fulfills his promises and in the fullness of time.

How long are we willing to wait on God? Abraham never possessed the promise of inhabiting the land. This didn't occur until the time of Solomon hundreds of years later! Very few of us will be that patient.

Prior to the vision experienced as recorded in chapter 17, Abraham and Sarah have been scheming about how to make a great nation. Since Sarah has not been specified as the mother of the nation, she and Abe decide to help God out. Woe to the man who has such an ego as to think he is helping out God! God in no way needs us to fulfill his will. God invites us into the work, but God can do this in the twinkling of an eye if he wishes.

In the midst of their scheming, Abraham and Sarah choose their handmaiden, Hagar, as a good surrogate mother. Thus Hagar moves from a position of service to a position of power.

Observations and Opportunities

Sarah and Abe are suddenly at odds with one another, swapping blame and pointing fingers. After some twists and turns, Ishmael is born to Hagar. The name "Ishmael" means "God hears," affirming for Hagar that God is concerned about her.

What great patience God has with us! In our foolish and impulsive behavior, God is yet patient with us. Abraham and Sarah can see only *their* way of fulfilling God's promise, and they make a mess of it. God is always gracious and loving. He affirms Hagar and re-emphasizes his covenant with Abraham. Abraham and Sarah are given new names and are "transformed" even as very old adults. Sarah will conceive a child!

Now Sarah is 90 years "young," and Abraham is 100. I can tell you there are some physical obstacles that would prevent that from happening! But what may seem impossible with man, God makes possible. And Abe's reaction (and probably ours too) is uproarious, falling-on-the-ground, tears-out-the-eyes laughter! But with God, all things are possible.

OPPORTUNITIES FOR DAILY LIVING

We need to laugh more! Sometimes we need to have rolling-on-the floor and tears-flowing-from-our eyes laughter. We need more than the polite snicker or the smile; we need a good belly laugh from time to time. Laughter is an inner condition, a stance or point of view that is a reaction to the absurd. While we laugh at a 100-year-old couple conceiving a son, we soon realize that God is the God of the impossible.

- What makes you laugh?
- How do you find joy in life?
- What is the role of laughter in your life?
- How does laughter keep you from taking yourself too seriously?
- What do you think makes God laugh?

Luke 15:7 says that God is overcome with joy at the return of a repentant sinner. Some say that God laughs when we tell God *our* plans!

- When have you seen evidence of God's laughter?

I think God laughs at some of the absurdity of our actions! Certainly, there is enough absurdity in our world today.

- What do you see in our world that God might be laughing at today?

God wants us to have joy. God wanted to fulfill the desires of the hearts of Abraham and Sarah. God wants to fulfill the joys of our hearts too.

- For what are you praying?
- What gift from God would fill you with overpowering joy and laughter?

PRAYER

Thank you, God, for the complete joy we have in knowing you and being known by you. Thank you for the miracles of your love that bring us to tears of joy and laughter! Amen.

Abraham and Isaac
Genesis 22

OPENING

How is your "faith-o-meter"? How do you go about evaluating your faith? Is your faith weak, strong, consistent, spotty?

God has his own methods of measuring faith. It varies with individuals. These days it is hard to get peoples' attention. But God still finds a way into our hearts. In today's lesson we see how he really grabs hold of Abraham's attention. Abe is a great soul who lives in a crude age. Human sacrifice is the custom among many nations, including the Canaanites among whom Abraham lives.

We might ask why this difficult story of human sacrifice is included in the Bible. It is to show the lengths to which Abraham's devotion would take him; to show us the depth of his faith in God; to show us that God is still in the "attention-getting'" business.

Abe has already given up his past for his God. He has given up his home, his family, his security. He has given up his other son, Ishmael. But he says to himself in response to God's test: "I see the Canaanites sacrificing their children for their god. How can I do less for my God? How can I show the depth of my faith to those around me?"

What would you do in this situation? What would your "faith-o-meter" say about you?

OBSERVATIONS ON THE TEXT

God's test comes to Abraham in a shocking fashion. Isaac is a beloved son. The depth of Abe's love for this boy is exceeded only by Abe's faith in God. The pain of this command from God is searing. But Abraham doesn't even question God. And look at the preparation he goes through for this one act. He cuts the wood (he has help with him). He prepares the place for the altar. Abraham could give lots of excuses to God. After all, he is more than 100 years old! But he doesn't waver a bit. This is quite a task, and yet Abe is faithful in his preparation and obedience. I don't think I could have been so faithful. What about you?

Isaac carries his own execution tools. Two thousand years later another son will carry his own execution instrument too. But Jesus would not ask, "Where is the lamb?" He already knew. Nor would Jesus return joyfully from his mountain as Isaac did.

Abraham has learned through his life that God can be counted on to provide. So he does not waver when God asks for the sacrifice of Isaac. Abraham trusts God to provide for him in this test too. As Isaac begins to question about the article for sacrifice, again Abe tells Isaac, "God will provide the lamb."

Can you imagine what that walk would have been like? . . . Abraham and Isaac on a walk across a mountain path; the father wrestling with his faith and the challenge to obey; the son, playful and engaged as only a young boy would be.

Do you think Abraham talked to Isaac about the way of faith as they hiked? What do you suppose they talked about as they walked? What would you have talked about with your child? In verses 10 and 11 we see that things suddenly get very tense. Can you imagine building an altar with your son, knowing that the child will be the sacrifice?

Agony and fear no doubt fill both the father and son as Abe binds Isaac and fits him on that altar. The quality of Abraham's faith is revealed in a powerful way. With his son tied to the altar, Abe takes out his knife and lifts it ready for the sacrifice.

There is fear and also an intimacy revealed here between Isaac and Abe and between Abraham and God. God's spirit calls out to Abraham, repeating his name over and over. As Abraham's knife is poised, ready to strike, God calls Abe's name. And then, in verse 12, we read that God stops this test. Did God not know how this would turn out? Why does Abraham have to be tested at such a horrible level?

The omniscient God has all knowledge, but Abraham has free will to choose. God does not interfere with man's will. Abraham has to prove that he does not love his child more than he loves God.

What would you have done in this situation? Thankfully, a ram is already there, caught in the thicket. God does exactly what Abraham has told Isaac on the way to the altar: "God will provide the lamb!" God also provides a great blessing to Abe: You and your family will be more than the stars in the sky. This is a happy ending for sure! God is not interested in death, but in life and in the depth of our obedience. God prevented the death of this beloved son. Years later he would not prevent the death of his own Son!

OPPORTUNITIES FOR DAILY LIVING

Later, Paul would pick up on the theme of sacrifice. In Romans 12:1 he exhorts us to present our bodies as "living sacrifices." God honored the human form when he sent his son in human form. Jesus could have taken any heavenly form, but God chose the human body. And God says to us, "I value your whole self—your body, your mind, your soul!"

- How are you presenting yourself as a living sacrifice?
- What shape is your soul in? Your mind?

We are living sacrifices when we are living witnesses. We are to represent God in all we do.

True worship of God is not liturgy, no matter how noble. Nor is true worship ritual, no matter how meaningful. True worship is offering to God one's total being every day. But before we can be useful laborers for Christ, we have to be transformed. Do you think Abraham and Isaac had a transformational experience that day?

As he did with Abraham, God looks for ordinary folks like you and me to help in the redemption of the world. Another lesson: Abraham learned that day that life is precious. When we believe we are owed everything, that we have a right to our own lives, we will be disappointed when things go wrong. It is only when we recognize that life is a gift we can celebrate no matter the challenge. Only then can you sing with me the old, old song: "Make me a blessing, make me a blessing. / Out of my life, may Jesus shine. / Make me a blessing, O Savior, I pray. / Make me a blessing to someone today!"

PRAYER

Make me a blessing, O God. Help me, like Abraham, to totally trust that you will indeed provide. And as I am transformed by my obedience and trust, make me a witness to others. Amen.

The heritage of Isaac
Genesis 24, 25:5-6

OPENING

I'm a native of Indiana, a Protestant state. Folks in Indiana are called "hoosiers," which is a "high falootin" name for "hillbilly." Hoosiers are a bunch of English-Scottish-Irish-German-Welsh-Dutch, all with three or more generations on this continent. In such a culture you would hardly expect to find many Roman Catholic or Jewish people.

The Jewish community was indeed small when I was coming up a hundred years ago, so scarce in fact that I was in the third grade before I ever saw a Jewish person. And, that incident was vividly impressed on me. Coming home from school one day, I saw a crowd of older children following a little stooped-over older man and calling him names like "Ikey" and "Sheenie." He had a long beard, a black coat, and a hat and was pushing a two-wheeled cart laden with tin ware and polishes. The kids were rough on him, but he trudged on without a response. Suddenly the school janitor appeared, protected the man, shamed the older kids, and shushed them to get home. That little Jewish man was the meekest, most unobtrusive person I had ever seen. I wondered why the Jewish man had been treated so badly, so I took the question home to my mother.

My mom told me about the people of Abraham, Isaac, and Jacob. She told me about how the Jewish people thought of themselves as God's chosen people—chosen by God, not as his pets or favorites as some suppose them to be even to this day. They were chosen from all the peoples of the earth to do a grand thing for all mankind: to give the world, through sorrow and tribulation, the Savior of the world—our Lord Jesus. Today we look at the heritage of Isaac, the son of this chosen promise.

OBSERVATIONS ON THE TEXT

Sarah was a unique woman for several reasons. She is the only woman in the Bible whose age is mentioned. This was not to embarrass her, but to emphasize her specialness. She was exceptionally beautiful, so much so that Abraham lived in fear that a neighboring king might try to cut off Abraham's head and take Sarah for his own. Sarah was an obedient wife; she made it known throughout the land that she was committed to Abraham for all eternity. However, she despaired at not being able to produce children, especially a son. So, she gave her handmaid to Abraham for childbearing. Who of us would have done such?

But then one day, at a very old age, Sarah delivered to Abraham a son. There were all the good makings of a television show here, with jealousy and multiple affairs. Yet, God's will prevailed. Isaac grew in favor with God and those around him. For 37 years Sarah trained Isaac to be a good, true, and loyal man. She watched him closely; some would say she was a "mother hen," an attitude that Abraham didn't like. And when Sarah died, Isaac was still unmarried—another thing that Abraham didn't like. It was the job of the mother to raise up her sons. The woman was to teach the boy how to be a man. Some of us need to hear this teaching today!

In Abraham's day the parents did the "matchmaking." The parents would negotiate, come to terms, and the girl would be delivered to her intended husband. The marriage was consummated if the man invited the girl inside his tent. That is the origin of the saying "I'll trade you, sight unseen." The girl's face was covered, and she didn't remove her veil until the young man offered the invitation to come in. Such a courtship has no appeal in our Western civilization. We want to see what we are "buying." Judging from the number of divorces nowadays, perhaps parents should be more involved in the courtship; and perhaps courting should be more about blending family values than about sexual attraction.

Abraham sent Eliezer, a most trusted servant, to find a Jewish wife for Isaac. He left Hebron with riches to show that Abraham had a son worthy of marriage. And, as Eliezer traveled, he prayed, "O God, I cannot succeed in this delicate mission unless you help me. Please grant me success in this today" (Gen. 23:12). Eliezer took the camels down for water where the women came to gather water. He used his own wit and his dependence upon God. When Eliezer first saw Rebekah, he knew God had answered his prayer. He then followed the traditions of his day and set up the union with Rebekah. And the rest is history!

OPPORTUNITIES FOR DAILY LIVING

When I was 16 I went to the Baptist church in the morning and the Methodist church in the evening, much to my father's disgust. One Sunday evening, I went for ice cream with another Methodist girl and two Methodist boys. I didn't get home until almost 10 o'clock. Coming home, I saw the lights in my home burning full blast. I knew something was up and, when I entered the house, my daddy sternly said, "Where have you been?" And I told him. Then he gave me a long lecture about a house divided against itself and finally ended the lecture with this admonition: "There are plenty of good boys in our Baptist church. You best pay attention to the Baptists." I took his advice and never regretted it. That's parental involvement!

At age 40 Isaac was depressed. His mother had died, his father was near death, his trusted servant Eliezer was away, and he was an old unmarried man. He was hoping that Eliezer would find him a suitable woman for marriage. Eliezer was praying the same thing. When the caravan returned, Rebekah and Isaac were captivated by each other, and they went into the tent and she became his wife. Too often in courtship no one else is brought in as counsel. Isaac and Rebekah found themselves caught up in lust but maybe not love. As our children seek love, let us give them good guidance and wise counsel.

Isaac received a good healthy heritage. His mother and father made sure he followed the ways of the Lord. Isaac was obedient in following the teachings of his tradition. He was a hard worker, a cattleman. (We here know what hard work that is!) What a blessing when a son follows in the footsteps of his father and shares in the good work. Isaac inherited all that was Abraham's (Gen. 25:5) and followed in the ways of the Lord. And in this long line of heritage between Isaac and Rebekah, we will see our Lord Jesus in their family tree.

- How are you being obedient, seeking counsel, and following good traditions?
- How is God blessing you and your children and your children's children?

PRAYER

O God, give me success today that I may be found faithful. Show your steadfast love to me and my family today so that I may do great things for your work and your world. Amen.

Jacob and Esau*
Genesis 27, 28

OPENING

Jacob was what we might call a "con man," and he was very successful at it. Esau had every right to be angry at losing his birthright. Esau lost a great inheritance, but he also lost the prestige of representing his family to God as a priestly intercessor. Esau was careless in his actions with a result that Jacob could not reverse. How many lives have been penalized by the carelessness of one word that cannot be "unsaid" or one deed that cannot be "undone"?

Deception did not originate with Jacob, but it became part of his operating mode when he went along with this mother's plan to steal the birthright. Rebekah may have thought she was carrying out the will of God. Had God not told her before the birth of the boys that "the elder shall serve the younger"? If she had dealt openly and honestly with Isaac, persuading him to give to Jacob that which was predestined to be his, she might have avoided all the pain. Instead, she incited a deceit that would set off a chain of lies, anger, exile, and death.

OBSERVATIONS ON THE TEXT

No one has ever loved his or her child too much. It was not the intensity of the affection for Jacob that was the problem; it was the interference with truth and duty that was wrong. Rebekah loved her son more than the truth. She loved her son more than she loved her husband and more than she loved God. Compare her love for Jacob with the love Abraham had shown for Isaac. Abraham was faithful first to God. Rebekah was faithful first to Rebekah.

To avoid the coming anger from Esau, Rebekah sends Jacob to her brother's house for "a few days." But the consequences of evil are often longer and more serious than one can foresee. We pick up Jacob's story in Genesis 28:10 when we see him weary, alone, and lonely. Perhaps until now Jacob has thought little about God, choosing to live by his own wits, in his own ways. Isn't this typical of the lost sinner, at the end of his tether, not seeing God but with God's moving toward him?

Weary and exhausted, Jacob falls asleep on a rock. He is not in an oasis or in a pleasant meadow; he is out in the middle of nowhere. The barrenness of this place seems to represent at that moment Jacob's heart and mind. And as he sleeps on his stone, he has a dream. (Not a dream like that of Martin Luther King Jr. No.) This is a dream about a ladder, a stairway to heaven, with angels ascending and descending. Jacob does not deserve a vision from God, but he needs it. We can relate, can't we? We too sometimes feel like spiritual exiles— poor, lonely, traveling through what seems like an empty land. And then God shows up!

God takes the initiative to meet Jacob's need. God always shows up in unexpected ways and in unexpected places. We may have a tendency to localize God to certain places such as the church and to certain times like Sundays. We need to correct that idea. God has contact with more than religious and righteous people. There is just no telling where or how God might confront us. We cannot predict that.

Jacob is not a righteous man at this point, but God majors in using poor material. God says to Jacob, "No matter where you go, I will be there too." God is not confined to any one place or to any certain time. God is omnipresent; there is nowhere that God is not!

When a man is made to know that God has not forgotten him, even though he has been a moral failure, there is a moment of exultation much like that which Jacob experienced. Angels of God's forgiveness seemed to throw a bridge across the distance between Jacob and God. He was bowed in agonized unworthiness and God picked him up. In the same way, when we bow in agony and guilt and repentance, God picks us up. And, as Jacob awakes, he builds a sacred altar. He would never forget this place!

Have you ever had an unforgettable encounter with God so incredible that you never wanted to leave that place and that moment? Jacob memorializes his earth-shaking encounter with God. He has known about God before. I'm sure his father Isaac had told him the story of the sacrificial camping trip he'd taken with his own father, Abraham. I'm sure Isaac had told his sons over and over how God had provided a ram. Yes, Jacob has heard about God for years, but he probably has never really experienced God until now. Jacob comes to a personal experience with God, to know who God is and what God wants to do through him. Suddenly his awareness is expanded, his life is transformed, and he begins a whole new lifestyle. So it is with us when we come to personally experience the living God. We too are transformed, and life begins anew!

OPPORTUNITIES FOR DAILY LIVING

When life's struggles become real in a man and he turns to God, a man is worthy of his life and can begin to make a difference.

- How did you become aware of God in your life?
- What difference has knowing God made in your life?
- How do you stay aware of God's love for you?
- How do you stay obedient to God's will for your life?

Jacob made a "profession of faith." He embraced a deep personal relationship with God and became aware of the obligations of his commitment. As our faith grows, so our commitment strengthens. Our serving and giving will be our response to God's undeserved blessings.

- How is God strengthening you?
- How are you responding?

Human nature has changed little over time. The path of struggle for Jacob is in a sense everyone's struggle. We are all travelers from birth through life. God is available to us, with us, and providing for us.

PRAYER

If, God, you will be with me, then I shall continue serving you faithfully—in good times and in not-so-good times. O God, be with me in all of my days as your obedient disciple. Amen.

At the end of this lesson Eula Mae had hand-written these words: "I should not be teaching this class according to the thoughts of some." She didn't finish the response, but I get the feeling she would have said, "If God will be with me and keep me, I shall continue faithfully!" That was her spirit! Perhaps that might become ours as well.

Jacob and Laban
Genesis 31

OPENING

Think about your best friend in the world. What one word describes your relationship? Think about your most troubled relationship. What one word describes this relationship?

Relationships with others affect every aspect of our lives—how we act, how we feel, even how we see God. Some people can't stand to be poor. They become envious and bitter if someone else has something they want but cannot afford. Some cannot live without an adoring group of friends. They need others to keep them feeling important and like a celebrity. Some desire fame and fortune. They want it all! Yet, most of us really need an attitude change or at least an attitude review. Change your attitude to a more positive outlook and you can change your life. Let's look at an episode of changed attitudes today.

OBSERVATIONS ON THE TEXT

After Jacob had cheated Esau out of his birthright, he fled to his uncle, Laban, in Haran. Laban had agreed to give one of his daughters as Jacob's wife in exchange for seven years of labor. Jacob was smitten with Rachel, a living doll, but Laban tricked Jacob. On the marriage night Jacob found himself with Leah, Rachel's less attractive sister. Jacob has to spend another seven years working for Laban in order to have the love of his life, Rachel.

Afterward, Jacob decides to leave Haran and return home. This meant that assets have to be divided. Laban is still up to his devious tricks but, protected by God, Jacob's wealth increases—which creates mounting envy in the family. The sons of Laban see their father as dimwitted, weak, and favoring his daughters. They refuse to accept that the family's good fortune has come from the hard work of Jacob. Envy leads to anger and division. In the midst of the conflict Jacob figures it is time to head home, even though memories of home are not safe and warm. Even with all that Jacob has endured there, he is ready to go home.

Rachel and Leah are obedient wives. They too feel the growing confrontation with their brothers. They both also feel the deception by their father, realizing that he does not have their interests at heart, but is focused only on his own self-interests. He kept their dowries for himself instead of establishing a heritage for them. He is deceptive. Deception rules the household of Laban. In fact, when Jacob and his brood leave, it is three days before Laban is made aware. Some family! So, Laban does what any good overbearing father would do: he chases them down. Along the way, God warns Laban to be careful of what he says to Jacob.

Laban says that he only wants to kiss his daughters and grandchildren goodbye. Yet, Jacob does not trust anything Laban has to say. Once trust is violated, is lost, how can it be regained?

Jacob pays attention; Jacob trusts God; Jacob has a rightness within him that is stronger than his ambition. It would serve many of us well to examine our ambitions, our character, and our dreams.

Romans 13:13 reminds us that we are to walk honestly and not in contention or with envy. We are to live with a transparent integrity that results from an inward discipline of putting on the character of Jesus Christ. Jacob, over his years, had begun living into this admonition. I'm not sure Laban ever did! However, the story ends with Jacob and Laban building a covenant, erecting an altar, and agreeing to live in a new relationship going forward. They do this not only for one another; they do this in the eyes of God. God will be the "watchman" between the two of them in their agreement. The covenant is fair. The trouble begins with envy and deceit. The story ends with changed attitudes between a father and a son-in-law. God indeed changes attitudes. The first verses of Genesis 32 say, "Jacob went on his way and the angels of God met him."

I'm not sure I could have forgiven Laban or kept working to help build his business enterprises. But Jacob was God's man, and his attitude impacted the attitudes of many others. What about us?

OPPORTUNITIES FOR DAILY LIVING

Thomas Wolfe said, "You can't go home again!" Most of us have been blessed and hurt by the past, and many of us sometimes have the urge to "run back home to Mommy and Daddy." We cannot reject the memories of the past any more than we can predict the events of the future. We love home. We love going home. And you *can* go home again; just don't expect home to be like it was when you left! We can't reverse the flow of time.

- What are some of your favorite memories of home?
- Who was your best friend when you were growing up?
- If you could go home again, would you? Why or why not?

Christianity is about relationships. Christianity is a covenant. We have to be reminded continually that our faith is a covenant between God and us. Christianity is not built upon a creed. Jesus affirmed this when he said that the first and greatest commandment was between us and God and that the second was just as important—a relationship to our neighbors.

There are those in our world who are trying to set up God as a judge to be appeased by our following the right rules. But never forget that even when we fall short, God still loves us. The covenant is now and will always be in place, regardless of what some would have us believe. We must pay more attention to our relationships with God and with others. This cannot be done in vengeance; this cannot be done in cowardice; this can only be done in courage. And we must be steadfast in a courageous faith that keeps the covenant.

Let us not belittle our humanity. God honored humanity by becoming human. As humans, we model ourselves after God. And, God is the God of change. God is always bringing change to us—changes for the better. We are the ones who pervert change and cause the problems we must confront. Let truth rule. Let us be followers of Jesus and children of God. Honest people sharing honest truths never fear differences of opinion. Honesty begets truth. It doesn't mean that we will always agree, but it does mean that we can always trust one another to deal honestly and sincerely without hidden agendas, lies, or working for personal gain at the expense of others. Like Laban, many of us need changed attitudes.

- What will it take for you to have changed attitudes?

PRAYER

God, forgive me when I have tried to put myself before others. Forgive me when I've held on to negative attitudes so that I might profit. Help me, O God, to change my attitudes, to honor your covenant, to love you and my neighbors for the betterment of the world. Amen.

Joseph and his brothers
Genesis 42–45

OPENING

A traveler with time on her hands between flights at the airport bought a small package of cookies and sat down in the busy snack shop to read her paper. As she read, she became aware of a rustling noise and was shocked to see a well-dressed gentleman sitting across from her, helping himself to her cookies. Half-angry and half-embarrassed, she gently reached over and slid the package closer to her and began to munch on another of her cookies. A minute or so passed before she heard the man reaching for another cookie. By now, there was only one cookie left. Finally, as if to add insult to injury, the man broke the one remaining cookie into two pieces, pushed one half across the table toward her with a frown, and gulped down his half. He left without even saying thank you. She sat there dumbfounded!

A little later when her flight was announced, the woman opened her handbag to get her ticket ready. To her shock, there in her purse was her package of unopened cookies! Somewhere in the airport, there was a puzzled gentleman trying to figure out how that strange woman could have been so forward and so selfish.

Life can be looked at from a variety of understandings. Today we are looking at how one man coped with some unusual circumstances of his life. There is hardly a better example of how to deal with circumstances that we do not choose than Joseph.

OBSERVATIONS ON THE TEXT

We find it hard enough to accept blows that come to us through sickness, accidents, or shifts in the stock market. Joseph had been instilled with the values of his parents. They taught him well about the ups and downs of life. Jacob knew that bad news was always coming. Jacob also knew that there would always be good news following. There was famine in Canaan, but there was food in Egypt. He also knew that, if his family were to survive, his sons would have to help get food.

Isn't that often how God works? Life is a perennial interaction of events and responses. Joseph's brothers struck out with evil. Joseph would repay their evil with kindness. The brothers were envious of Joseph and his imaginative pronouncements. They sold him for 20 pieces of silver—the price of a "not so good" slave. Resentment perverts a person's thinking, vexes his spirit, and corrupts his actions. Resentment is destructive both to the one who hates and to the one who is hated. But we are commanded to not repay evil with evil. As far as it depends on you, live at peace with everyone.

We must always be open to new opportunities. The brothers sold Joseph into slavery in Egypt. From the wreck of his "good life" in Canaan, Joseph finds himself in the chains of slavery and in prison. But rather than brood and feel sorry for himself, we see Joseph learning a new language and adopting new customs. He builds himself up through a series of new relationships. We see him using his God-given intuition to bring good to the king to whom he is enslaved. This builds trust and leads to Joseph's being put into a place of high leadership. He is chosen by the king to be the one to rule over the land of Egypt, a phenomenal rise from prison to the palace.

Could you have done all that Joseph did? Could you have used your gifts for good to rise to new levels of leadership? Isn't it wonderful how God gives us the opportunities to rise from our challenges? God's goodness just keeps coming and coming.

Joseph's brothers appear before him in the court. This is perhaps the biggest test for Joseph. His brothers come to buy grain for their starving families in Canaan. The brothers don't recognize Joseph, but he recognizes them. He chooses to set aside revenge for the love of his family. Three times he calls them "spies." Then he charges them to prove they aren't by sending one of the brothers back to their home to get their youngest brother: "If you don't do this, I'll know you are spies." He is formulating a plan by which he can help his brothers and reunite himself with his father. The story has a happy ending. He reveals himself to his brothers: "I am Joseph, your brother." And their reunion is ultimately a happy one.

OPPORTUNITIES FOR DAILY LIVING

Guilt destroys the soul. Joseph's brothers had dealt with their deceit for years. They had to continually cover up the lie they had told their father. While they seemed to have a good life, the guilt ate at them. One of the worst sins we have to deal with is hard-heartedness. Guilt turns us hard toward others as well as toward God. The brothers recognized their sinful nature. Joseph could have repaid their guilt with revenge, but his heart had changed too. He had matured from the spoiled little brat he was as a child.

- What guilt are you holding onto?
- To whom do you need to ask forgiveness?
- How have you matured?
- How has your maturity helped you clear away your guilt and soften your heart?

Joseph too had the opportunity to enact revenge, but he refrained. His maturity had brought him to the point of a loving and accepting attitude toward those who loved him and who had done him wrong. Think on this for a minute:

- Upon whom would you like to bring revenge?
- How have they hurt you?
- How would you like to repay them?

Viktor Frankl, an Austrian psychiatrist, was imprisoned by Hitler in World War II. While in the concentration camp Frankl observed some prisoners caring for some of the others who were near death, sharing a sip of water or a crumb of bread. He became aware that everything a man has can be taken from him—everything, that is, but the ability to choose his own attitude in any set of circumstances. Circumstances do not make us. Our attitudes to those circumstances do.

- What is your attitude saying to you today?

PRAYER

God, help me, help me, help me! There is so much around me that I would like to respond to with revenge and hurt. Help me, help me, help me to let your heart be my heart. Amen.

Balancing obedience and relationships
Exodus 20:1-20

OPENING

The Ten Commandments are perhaps some of the most beloved verses of the Old Testament. God gave these laws to Moses for the good of the children of Israel. God must have thought laws were important since God and Moses spent a lot time talking about them (see Deut. 6:1-12). Throughout history, faith groups of all types acknowledge that God desires order from chaos and a common moral way of life.

Moses was instructed in a similar way to bring order out of the 40 years of wandering in the wilderness. The Ten Commandments were God's way of helping Moses sort out the complicated relationships and to bring order to the chaos that was Israel. God said: "Write it on your heart and your doorposts." The purpose of this practice was to remind God's people that God's law was something to be ever aware of, to be carried in their hearts and minds, so that they would behave appropriately. They were daily reminders of how to interact with God and with one another. These commandments were a guide—not an ornament!

The giving of these commandments is really when the redeeming work of the Christ began to be fashioned. As soon as Moses brought the commandments down from God, the children of Israel had already taken life into their own hands. God makes it so simple for us, but we always seem to find ways to complicate things. I find that one good way to understand the Ten Commandments is to read them as a prelude to the Sermon on the Mount. God is always trying to call us back to obedience.

OBSERVATIONS ON THE TEXT

The laws given are for our benefit. God doesn't want us to obey his commandments simply because he said so. He wants us to be obedient because he loves us, and these are life lessons for our benefit. Obedience will bring us more joy, a longer life, deeper relationships, and a more prosperous life. There are some really practical angles here if only we will pay attention.

Keeping the Sabbath helps us to relax and rest. If we honor our parents and neighbors, God brings great joy. Keeping things and thoughts in proper perspective brings happiness. We have to obey with the right attitude. It is easy for us to measure others by God's law, but easier still for us to rationalize away our shortcomings.

We are like the farmer who prided himself on being a pretty good man. He bragged about being pretty good, about average he supposed. One day he sent his hired hand out to build a fence. When the hand returned that day, he reported, "I built a pretty good fence today. There are good places and some bad places. I guess it's about an average fence." The farmer challenged him: "Don't you know a fence has to be perfect or it's not much good at all?" "Well," said the hand, "I used to think so till I heard you averaging out things with the Lord!"

We cannot settle for "about average" where God is concerned. The law was given to us through his love for us and for our well-being. It is our job to observe these commandments out of our love and desire to honor and please God.

Not only are we called to obey the law; we are also called to preserve it from generation to generation. We are to teach it in our homes and to represent it in our culture. God's laws are perhaps as important for a nation as civil laws. If we trace the problems in our country to their roots, most could be cured if only we followed this set of commandments. I know there are some modern-day ramifications, but following these would solve a lot of our problems. God uses every method to impress us with the importance of obedience—keeping his law for the right reasons, with the right attitude, from generation to generation.

1. Have no other gods: Seek first the kingdom of God. Love God fully.
2. Have no graven images: God is Spirit. God is neither confinable nor controllable.
3. Don't take God's name in vain: Even the very name of God is holy and not controllable.
4. Honor the Sabbath: This is for our benefit to give us rest and refreshment.
5. Honor your parents: They brought us into life through love. Return the love to them.
6. Don't kill: Don't even hate. Honor your neighbors.
7. Don't commit adultery: Keep your eyes to yourself. Don't look, desire, or lust!
8. Don't steal: Give away what you have to the poor. Give when you are asked.
9. Don't bear false witness: Speak the truth. Be honest. Build a trustworthy reputation.
10. Don't covet anything or anyone: Hold others in high esteem, and love one another.

OPPORTUNITIES FOR DAILY LIVING
- What part of your life and your relationships needs the law?
- Which commandment do you most appreciate? Why?
- Which commandment do you least appreciate? Why?
- How does obedience of these commandments enhance your freedom?

These commandments outline the vertical and horizontal relationships in our lives. Vertical is to God: Worship only him in spirit. Reflect this reverence of the holy in speech and life. Regularly and reverently remember to keep this relationship vital. Horizontal is to others: Be a testimony to a strong family and marriage. Keep your emotions in check and live honestly, keeping communication clear; control your ambitions and desires.

- Which challenges you the most: the vertical relationship or horizontal relationship?
- What might you need to do to strengthen these?

PRAYER
O God, my God, help me to remember that my relationships with you and with others are holy and sacred. Help me have the strength to live as you have commanded. Remind me gently, Lord, when I step beyond the boundaries. Thank you for being the perfect parent to us all, loving us unconditionally and eternally. Amen.'

I am the Lord your God
Exodus 20:2-6

OPENING

We are torn in many directions these days. We are torn by our love for things of this world while also grasping for the spiritual things. We try in vain to hold on to both, to live in both worlds. But we know it is futile. Jesus reminds us that no one can serve two masters, and yet we still try. Many of us think we can control God. We give him our "shopping list," hoping he will fulfill everything we ask. Others of us think we can control ourselves and the people around us. We are heavy-handed and hard-hearted, only to find ourselves in all sorts of pain.

God said to Moses, "Your people are headed to prosperity; this land of promise is rich and productive." But Moses and the children of Israel could not grasp this blessing. The way they lived—or wanted to live—was more important than what God had provided. God brought this first commandment to them so they would remember the priority relationship in their lives.

So much like them are we! We think that we can live as we please and show up occasionally and God will wipe our slates clean. We've made living so complicated. But God told Moses as he tells us today, "Here are 10 simple rules for living a good life. These will never be repealed or replaced. They will never become outdated. Follow these rules and prosper." . . . If only we could!

OBSERVATIONS ON THE TEXT

This first commandment could have been simply, "Thou shalt believe in me as God." Or this could have been a law against atheism. God took care of all that in creation. We don't teach a baby to hunger or thirst. We are born with instincts. And we instinctively believe and worship something. But we soon discover that no false god will ever satisfy the longing of our souls. We have to be told and constantly reminded that the Lord God is our God and that we shall have no other gods. Too many things get in the way of this relationship. We must discipline ourselves through prayer and supplication to keep God at the forefront of our lives.

Many people squander their lives searching for an earthly satisfaction that will never be fulfilled. The cemeteries are filled with people who wasted their lives for nothing. If only they could have listened to Jesus and reordered their priorities . . .

There are five objects of our "false" worship: wealth, fame, pleasure, power, and knowledge.

Most of us are never satisfied with what we possess. Our dissatisfactions obscure God, and our search for things diverts us from our search for God.

We are all born wanting to be known. Many people wreck their lives simply because they haven't had the attention they crave.

In seeking happiness, we are often fooled to believe that it comes from physical pleasure. Pleasure is a drug whose dosage must by constantly increased in order for us to be fulfilled.

Power is a "kissin' cousin" to pleasure. We think that the more things we can control, the more special we are. Seeking power is another drug that never satisfies.

The more we think we know, the less obedient we are to what we really know. The search for knowledge keeps us from ever living by faith.

God continually reminds us of his provisions for us. Everything we have ever needed has been provided by God. Yet too many of us seek what is forbidden or what is hurtful in the search for life's treasures. God is not our enemy, making arbitrary decisions about what is harmful. God already knows what is best for us and what is harmful. God wants us to have life and to have it more abundantly within the boundaries he has set for us. The problems come when we get "too big for our britches" and begin thinking that we are our own god and that we know better than our heavenly father.

God makes it clear that we are to make no idol or image of God. Why not? Because the artist soon thinks that if he can make a representation of God, he can control God. Any article that can be made by man can be turned into an article of devotion. Many people worship money. Others worship art or other icons and images. God says explicitly that all idols soon fall flat in trying to represent the brilliance and magnificence of God.

OPPORTUNITIES FOR DAILY LIVING
- What idols get in the way of your relationship with God?
- What can you do to stay focused on God as your God?

On one side of a sheet of paper, list all the things God has provided for you. On the other side of the paper, list all the things you have provided for yourself.

- Which list is longer? What does that tell you?

We tell ourselves falsehoods so that we might pursue our own pleasures and actions. But God has given so much more to us than we have given ourselves that sooner or later we understand that chasing our own way is futile. Only God fulfills the deep longing of our soul.

True wisdom leads a person to take an inventory of his life before God does.

- If you were to stand before God today, would you be pleased with your presentation? Would God be pleased?

True worship is when we are in fellowship with God. This is a good day for making some shifts.

PRAYER
God, forgive my arrogance. Forgive my straying. Forgive me when I think more of myself than I think of you. Keep me focused on the goodness that only comes from you. Keep me in right relationship with you so that I might stay in right relationship with myself and others. Amen.

Do not take the name of the Lord in vain
Exodus 20:8

OPENING
General Orders
August 3, 1776

The General is sorry to be informed that the foolish and wicked practice of profane cursing and swearing, a vice hitherto little known in our American Army, is growing into fashion. He hopes that the officers will, by example as well as influence, endeavor to check it and that both they and the men will reflect that we can little hope of the blessing of Heaven on our army if we insult it by our impiety and folly. Added to this it is a vice so mean and low without any temptation that every man of sense and character detests and despises it.

Signed,
George Washington, General

How unfortunate that for many people, God is the object of worship on Sunday and the subject of profanity on Monday. We come in humility to worship, then we go to work with irreverence. Profanity is not the cause but the result of a deeper disease. That disease is blasphemy.

When we use God's name to give dignity and force to an unholy purpose, we have blasphemed the Lord our God. Just as some have tried to justify the liquor industry, gambling, and slavery with the use of Scripture, another vice that tears down instead of builds up is blasphemy. When we do this, we disgrace the holy name of God. Let us strive to do better.

OBSERVATIONS ON THE TEXT

Why is God so concerned with those who will misuse God's name? God wants us in loving relationship with him. God wants us to honor him and live in the sacred. When we are profane, when we speak stupidly in profanity, we pervert our own selves. Oaths insure the truth of a statement. We don't need the name of God attached to an oath if we are honest and trustworthy. Likewise, we don't need to use the name of God in profanity just to make a point. Too many of us also give false credit to the Lord when we are the ones who really want something to happen.

There are people who tell us, "The Lord led me to do such and such." Or there are those who say, "The Lord did this and told me such." What this kind of empty familiarity really means is, "I did such and such!" Then they blaspheme the Lord. This trap of insincerity and arrogance will not be tolerated by God.

Your mouth betrays your character. The tongue must be bridled! Psalm 141:3 and James 3:1 warn against that which comes from our mouths. Today, there is a noticeable lack of reverence for God's name. This reflects a similar lack of reverence for persons and has several results.

Filthy language reflects a lack of reverence for the holy. This is carelessness, a lack of personal discipline, and a general disregard for self and others. Use of religious formulas without any meaning is a cavalier attitude in which one seeks to explain away his own bad actions by blaming God. This is also an arrogance in which one takes upon one's self "blessing others" as if they are God.

A too-familiar attitude with God reduces the omnipotent, omniscient holy God to simply another idol. God is not "the man upstairs" or "the big boss." This too smacks of arrogance and a lack of sincere adoration of God, the author and finisher of all history.

Positively stated, we must use God's name in a sincere and earnest way. When we speak of God, we must do so in ways that communicate awe and an awareness of the great mystery of God. None of us can know the totality of the greatness of God. The psalmist said that words are inadequate to try to describe his majesty. So, what makes us think we can?

OPPORTUNITIES FOR DAILY LIVING

Many of us have learned "cuss words" from an early age. We may have heard these words in a back room or in the "barnyard." For many of us, we simply laugh this off and keep going. Yes, profanity leaves a mark on the innocent. And, when allowed to continue, this behavior can scar young minds and lead to terrible actions. The Christian has the obligation to confront this behavior in much the same way that General Washington did.

- How can you confront the use of profanity?
- How often do you appoint God as the author or scapegoat of your bad choices?

I've sat through too many church businesses being told that "the Lord led" when I knew that the Lord did nothing of the sort! This is just as blasphemous as taking the name of the Lord in vain. False oaths do not help your reputation or prove your trustworthiness. If a man is not big enough to take responsibility for his own actions, he is not worth following. People who do the right thing for the right reasons and assign the right appropriation to God are the ones I want to follow.

- Who are some effective Christian leaders that you appreciate?

PRAYER

You are such a magnificent Lord. I feel unworthy to speak your name. I am grateful for your love for me. I am thankful that you know my name. And I am overwhelmed with humility that you not only hear my prayers, but also act on them. Thank you, O God, for your love for me and so many others. Amen.

Remember the Sabbath
Exodus 20:8-11

OPENING

Everything about God's universe is orderly. God began with chaos and then organized everything into perfect arrangement. All of nature complements itself; everything fits together until disturbed by man. Man's emotional and spiritual world was in good order until Satan persuaded man that he was smarter than God.

The Ten Commandments were given to help man bring order back to himself both personally and spiritually. All of God's divine laws play a part in renewing fellowship between God and man. We are God's subjects. We must meet God's standards—not the other way around. We must please God. So, let's hear these commandments again and hear what God is calling us to today.

OBSERVATIONS ON THE TEXT

What is a Christian to do on Sunday? Most of us are gloriously inconsistent, condemning one practice while we indulge in another. The Sabbath was made so that we would rest. The early rabbis would say, "Stop doing what you normally do for a while." What is the difference between what you do on Sunday and what you do on Monday?

The Sabbath was made as a reward for labor. When a man labors, not for a livelihood but only for accumulating wealth, he is a slave to his labor. The Sabbath was a way to proclaim that Jews are free and not slaves. The Sabbath shows the relationship of man to God. After laboring, God rested. We are to do the same. Worship is a daily matter. The Sabbath is not a time to do nothing; it is a time to change our priorities.

Observing the Sabbath is serious business. In Exodus 31:12-15, God emphasizes the importance of this directly to Moses. In other references this is to imply a day of rest, a day of communing with God, a true indication of commitment to God and part of the covenant between God and man. God is serious in wanting this to be a holy day, a day of rest, a day of reordering one's self in relationship to God and to family and neighbor.

The Old Testament answers the question of how the Sabbath was instituted, but it takes the New Testament to fully explain why and to give more understanding on what is lawful. By this time the "law" had become more of a burden than a blessing. The Pharisees had written more than 1,500 conditions as to what one could not do on the Sabbath. For example, a person was not permitted to pin on a ribbon, pluck a gray hair, or even reap a handful of grain. The people were bound by the letter of the law and missed the spirit of it. Jesus, weary of the absurdity and hypocrisy, pushed back. The Sabbath was made for man!

We have Pharisees among us today too. There are those who are more concerned with the legalistic meanings than the spiritual freedom. Jesus would continue to preach flexibility but remained steadfast in the underlying principles of the faith. He opposed the man-made traditions that sought to restrict our freedoms in faith. Doing good is sometimes complex in our society. But the truth remains: Not to do good when it is in our power to do so is evil!

What conclusions can we draw from Jesus on this commandment? He did not regard physical exertion as desecrating the Sabbath. The Sabbath was not meant to depress or enslave us, but to free us and lift our souls. The Sabbath was meant to be a day of joy, praise, and time with family—not a day of depression or restriction. Jesus rejected the legalistic restrictions but did not reject the command to honor the Sabbath. Jesus would agree that if doing good on the Sabbath requires a sweat, we should sweat!

We cannot force people to worship or to keep the Sabbath holy. God does not want men to come to church because the golf course is closed! God wants us in relationship and communion with him and others because this is our heart's desire. God also does not approve of our feeling superior because we might keep the Sabbath, come to church, or otherwise honor this day. We have the personal responsibility to seek God, to magnify the Lord, and to do things for the benefit of others. This can happen on the Sabbath as well as on any other day of the week.

OPPORTUNITIES FOR DAILY LIVING

We are free every day to decide how we will live. If going to the movies or a sporting event brings us pleasure, we should go. And, as we go, we are to magnify God with our Christian witness.

- How are you representing God as you go about your daily work, play, and relationships?
- How are you representing God in your life on Sunday?
- What is the difference between how you live on Sunday and how you live the other days of the week?

How do we justify our inconsistencies in living out our faith? How do we condemn stores for being open on Sunday and all the while going shopping on Sunday? When do our ministers get to take their Sabbath? (They have to work on Sundays.)

- How often do your criticisms come back to "bite you"?
- Who is the Lord of your Sabbath?
- What do you do to keep the Sabbath holy?
- What do you do if you "need" to work on Sunday?

We need Sunday to lift us out of the daily grind. Even the miner lets his mules spend a day outside in fresh air and good sunlight! We need this time to remind us of who we are and whose we are. We need to rest because we are so fragile. This is possibly the easiest of the commandments to keep, and yet often we don't.

- What chaos are you wrestling with that needs the orderly guidance of God?
- What fragile aspect of your life needs "Sabbath attention"?

PRAYER

Thank you, God, for a day to rest, to worship and to give ourselves a break from our daily chores. Forgive us for not taking advantage of this gift. Help us to take better care of our spiritual lives and our emotional lives, as well as our physical lives. Help us to honor you more. Amen.

You shall not covet
Exodus 20:17

OPENING

There is no law in the Ten Commandments like this 10th commandment. No American law says, "Thou shalt not be selfish!" This is a uniquely personal command, reflecting a whole philosophy of life. This is a life motivation, a life discipline to keep one's self in check so as to not want for more.

In the Greek, the word picture of *covet* is to "reach for more than you can grasp." The idea here is grasping or panting for something with overwhelming desire. Our whole society and economy are built upon this. Every advertisement, preview, or commercial is meant to make us want something we don't have—and, in many cases, something we don't need and will never be able to afford.

What would it take to satisfy you in material wealth? What is your idea of a successful person? Perhaps we need a new philosophy of success. Perhaps we need to understand that it is not wrong to want better things, just as it is not wrong to want a better life. What is wrong is being moved with desire for something or someone so much that we take it or them without regard for anything else.

The emotion of coveting is a very subtle sin. It has great destructive power. It can distort all of our life's values and become such a consuming passion that it crushes everything near and dear to us.

No one is immune from covetous behavior. Every generation is filled with this destructive power. The Bible is filled with example after example from the garden of Eden to the end of John's revelation. This 10th commandment is given to keep us on constant guard. Rather than being focused on the dark desires of our hearts, God tells us to stay in tune to the Holy Spirit so that love and generosity might be our guide.

OBSERVATIONS ON THE TEXT

It seems the more we get, the more we desire. There is no limit to what the craving of material possessions can do to destroy a soul. If we are not careful, we will be consumed by our wants and will stoop to anything in order to grasp what we desire. Perhaps the best example is the story of David and Bathsheba.

Yes, Bathsheba was a beautiful woman. Yes, David fixated on her. David's sin went beyond covetousness to murder and to almost professional, personal, and spiritual ruin. David had everything but was willing to sacrifice it all. Covetous behavior is like falling into quicksand. There is no way out but down.

Too many of us want what we want *now!* We are not willing to wait upon the Lord. We want what we want right now, and nothing will stop us from getting it. We tell ourselves false stories: "I deserve it. I've been a good person and I deserve this as my reward." "I'm worth it. I've done good work and been passed over in the past. Not this time!" Too many of us confuse our "wants" with our "needs." We need very little.

All of these are false messages that lead to ruin. Notice that covetous behavior always begins with "I" messages. If you find you are telling these messages to yourself, slow down the train. Or, the ride you may find yourself on will be more than you bargained for.

It is not wrong to enjoy the fruits of one's labor. Neither is it wrong to enjoy the spoils that have come your way. The problem comes when we think we are entitled to anything we want without doing the hard work and the respectable labor to achieve it. Make time for pleasure; make time to enjoy the life you are making. Just don't get caught up in the life someone else is making.

Take inventory of your physical and spiritual blessings. Include in your inventory a "wish list." What are the things in life you would like to work for? What are some relationships in your life that you would like to grow to be deeper? What in your spiritual life needs improvement?

When we are keeping an eye on our own selves and what we are continuing to strive for, we have less time to keep an eye on our neighbor, our neighbor's stuff, or our neighbor's spouse!

OPPORTUNITIES FOR DAILY LIVING

There comes a time in most of our lives when we need a review of our basic values of life. Doing this on an annual basis can keep us focused more on our own lives and less on the lives of others.

- What have you not achieved that you want to achieve?
- What does success look like to you?
- How do you know when you are achieving as you wish?
- What is out there that might tempt you to get off track?
- What "I" messages are you giving yourself?

If you are giving yourself positive affirmations and challenges, you are probably on the right track. If you are giving yourself the three negative messages of "I want," "I deserve," or "I'm worth it," you might need to reevaluate your life goals and values.

The opposite of covetousness is contentment. The Scriptures are filled with verses about staying within the boundaries of contentment. Perhaps Paul gave us the most famous of these in his words to the Philippians: "I have found in whatever state I am to be content" (Phil 4:11).

How does one reach a state of contentment? Well, that is the question we will wrestle with all of our lives!

A young lawyer was being interviewed by a junior partner in a prestigious New York law firm. The junior partner said, "Soon, you may be like me. I've just moved into a Park Avenue apartment with eight bathrooms!" The young lawyer instead came home to practice law in his small town. When asked why, he said, "Because I had no idea why I would want to work so hard so that I could have eight bathrooms!"

The most important moment in our lives may well be when we decide what it is we really want out of life and commit to that.

PRAYER

God, help me to stay focused on the priorities you have set for me. You have blessed me in ways I could never have imagined. Help me to learn the art of contentment. Amen.

Stand tall and look good
Psalm 1

OPENING

God made us to be productive. It is hard to imagine that any totally unproductive person can be fulfilled and happy. Those rooted in the spirit of God, living in God's power, produce fruit of God's spirit in behavior and attitude. Orange trees produce oranges, avocado trees produce avocados. Christians produce love, joy, peace, longsuffering, patience, gentleness, goodness, faith, meekness, and temperance (Gal. 5:22-23).

It's the happy life, the consistent Christian doing his thing quietly, naturally that we desire. The result: "Whatsoever he does will prosper." God will prosper his own in the direction he wants us to go.

Today we're examining Psalm 1, and we'll be trying to find out how to live a happy life and to be able to SING about our happiness.

OBSERVATIONS ON THE TEXT

(vv. 1-3) We will be happy when we follow the teachings of God. We are happy when we delight in the law of the Lord and meditate on this day and night. Those who do so will be like trees that will never thirst and will always bear fruit. As we focus on God's teachings, there is no time to sit with the scoffers. When we do God's work, there is no time to be wicked. We are constantly being tempted. The tempter wants us to abandon our focus on God and not bear fruit, not do good, not follow God. But following the tempter does not bring happiness.

Think about it. Following the law of God is freedom. I know that sounds funny, but we know the boundaries. The ungodly have to live by rules, scores, referees, day after day dragging themselves out of bed to do more work that is meaningless and purposeless.

Following the law of God, there are no rules except the ones we know. We can go anywhere in life we wish within the framework of the law. No one is keeping score, and there are no referees because we know the boundaries. There is challenge, excitement, cooperation. Yes, sometimes there are bruises and disappointments; that's just part of life. But more, there are thrills, surprises, successes, and victory. As long as you live within the boundaries of the law, you are *free*. If you ignore the law, you are in for long days and longer nights.

There is no happier person than one who knows what he should be and when he hasn't been what he should be, and then he is forgiven. For those who follow God and live in the law, even when they fall short, there is forgiveness and a clean slate. For the ungodly who ignore the law, even when they think they do good, their work is meaningless.

The psalmist draws out a symbolic picture of the godly man. This man is gracious, stable, and prosperous with never-failing resources for happiness. The metaphor is of a tree, not just any tree but a tree with deep roots and ever-producing fruit. It is evergreen, ever-producing, and always prosperous. Trees and people are expected to do more than just stand tall and look good. The godly man stands tall, looks good, and produces good things.

(vv. 4-6) The psalmist warns the wicked: If you do wicked things, you will not prosper. For the ungodly, life will be empty and ugly. There will be no substance, and there will be nothing but pain.

The believer's joy has to have a tinge of pain when surrounded by the disenchanted, disobedient, disgruntled, and discouraged. If we are not careful, their negativity rubs off on us. Our job is to be ever so gentle with them and reach them with the love and joy of God. It is a natural part of our love to do good. Knowing what happiness is and where to find it will result in our being enriched and fulfilled and, hopefully, in some of the ungodly being transformed and redeemed. Jesus transforms; we are his witnesses.

It sometimes begins innocently and intermittently. We see the ungodly thinking they are happy and enjoying life. We see them playing the game of "faking it," and we are enticed. When we are faked into pursuing happiness, we are headed for trouble.

OPPORTUNITIES FOR DAILY LIVING

The sky is not falling. God is in control. Yet, the ungodly are constantly telling us that the sky is falling, that the world is coming to an end, that everything is falling apart. The ungodly tell us that since everything is about to come to an end, we had better enjoy life to the fullest to satisfy our selfish desires. Once we get sucked into that, we are in trouble.

- How do you keep from hearing the cries of the ungodly?
- How do you meditate on the law both day and night?
- What brings joy to your life?
- With whom can you share this joy?
- What happens to your joy when you share your joy?
- How do you respond to "fakers"?

When we are faking happiness, it is easy to tell. And faking happiness is *not* happiness. The ungodly are insecure and have to be showy and even overdone to look like they have everything when, in reality, they have nothing.

- When do you feel like faking happiness?
- What does this feel like?
- How does the law give you freedom?

I don't like living by rules. You all know that I like to push the laws to the limit. But again, I want to remind you that living by the law is freeing. Think of this like a football field. The law outlines the "out of bounds." We can run around all over that field, having the best time, living to the fullest. We have freedom. Just don't go out of bounds. In some ways it is like a return to Eden. Here is everything in the world: just don't go to the tree of knowledge. Some of us can't live with that kind of freedom. How about you?

PRAYER

Help us, oh God, to accept the gift of freedom that you give us through Jesus. Help us to be satisfied with the freedoms we have rather than lusting after the things we are not allowed. Forgive us when we fake happiness. Help us to live free, happily ever after, in Jesus. Amen.

Sing!
Psalm 8

OPENING

What would life be without music? Some say it is our fourth need: food, clothing, shelter, and MUSIC! It is indeed a great medium of communication. Music is an instrument of fellowship. When men sing together, something extraordinary happens. Sing! Music sets a mood. Sing when things aren't right. Sing when things seem great. Sing to bring consolation when in pain. Sing to put spirit, courage, and hope into the hearts of others.

I can imagine the psalmist sitting out in the dark staring in the great heavens. The psalmist was amazed at the world, the sun, the moon, the stars. What he knew about them was very small. Yet he knew that compared to the sun, moon, and stars he was very small. In the midst of all the universe, why would God pay attention to one insignificant man?

Do you realize the closest star to the earth is the sun, 93 million miles away? The nearest stars are more than 50 billion miles away. Astronomers estimate that in our galaxy there are more than 100 million galaxies. I can't comprehend that much space. I can't comprehend how light ever works being generated through space to get to us. What a world we live in! What a time to be alive with such a wonderful creator!

And yet, in the bigness of the universe, God knows us intimately, so intimately that God knows about every hair on our heads—or some of the hairs that used to be on some of the heads of you men!

OBSERVATIONS ON THE TEXT

God has done some amazing things in the world. The world is made for us and made for us to love the world. God has also done something amazing in making us. God made the world as a wonderful gift for us. God has made us as caretakers of the world. It is amazing that God has put it all into order and we are the benefactors of all God's goodness.

The psalms were the hymnbook of ancient Israel. They were collected over a period of years and used in worship in the temple at Jerusalem. I would love to have heard the tunes to those amazing hymns.

Why don't we praise God more often? Do we forget what God has done for us? Are our minds filled with such trivial nit-picking criticisms that we don't have room for God? Do we think we deserve more than God has given us? Or, is it that we simply don't know how to praise God?

The Hebrews praised God for everything. At every turn they were building altars or giving holy names to places where God had done something special. Praise was the main way that Israel talked to God.

We have become selfish. We feel entitled. We expect things from God. Perhaps we need to sing more, to stack up some more rocks, to pay attention to the holy in the skies and sing to the heavens.

Praise is worship. Praise is an echo of our relationship to God. An isolated Christian often loses his spiritual vitality and effectiveness. Private worship is sustained by corporate worship. In corporate worship we are energized and amazed. In corporate worship we are reminded that as insignificant as we may feel, we are not an accident in God's economy. Yes, the stars are fabulous. Yes, the sun and moon are fabulous. And, yes, you and I are just as significant. We note that God crowned man with glory and honor. We have a unique relationship to praise and to take care of what God has given us.

What is man? Darwin might see us as a monkey's orphan. Marx might view us as an economic tool. Freud might just see us as a bundle of sexual drives. But all of these are incomplete views of who we are.

More amazing than all the scholars who have studied mankind is the love that God has put inside us. We are made to love, to live in relationship with God and with one another. We are the only created part of God's plan that is meant to live in multiple relationships. And so, as we sing, as we worship, we dwell on the wisdom of God. We give to God our inadequacies, our weaknesses, our sins, and we SING! Because God inhabits our praise, as we sing, as we praise, God sits beside us, walks beside us, fills our hearts.

OPPORTUNITIES FOR DAILY LIVING

Lest we be absorbed in contemplating our own greatness, we focus on the greatness of God.

- How are you focusing on God?
- How are you praising God?
- How are you singing?
- What are your favorite hymns? What do they mean?
- How do you keep from focusing on yourself?
- Why is praise not a daily habit?

I challenge you to write a modern-day hymn. Think about the things around you and about how God is more than all of these. Praise God in your hymn and see what happens.

God has no spoiled children, but some of us are acting like it. We complain when it is too hot or cold. We complain when it is raining or when it is dry. We complain when the TV or radio isn't working. We are a bit spoiled!

In those times when you have felt that no one understood you or cared for you, you have moved too far away from God. Do you remember how God responded to Peter, to the blind, to the lepers, to the tax collectors? We are like these in some ways. And as God loved them and responded to them, God responds to us. And God responds to the sun and the moon and the stars. But most of all, God responds to us. And that is reason for singing.

PRAYER

Dear God, show us anew who you are and how to praise you in genuine response. Forgive us for being so wrapped up in ourselves that we have lost sight of the great purpose for which we have been created. Thank you for the honor of fellowship with you. Help us to sing! Amen.

A psalm of prayers
Psalm 119

OPENING

One would not think of using a computer textbook to learn how to operate a microwave oven. The result not only would be unproductive but also baffling. We need to approach the Bible in the same way. The Bible is not a manual for operating a computer or a microwave. The Bible is not a book of science or of history.

Most of the Bible appears to be the words of God addressed to mankind through the authors of the different books of the Bible. These are words of wisdom that are a manual on how to live in community with our neighbors, following the rule of law that God has ordained. These are the words that show us how God led the nation of Israel as his chosen nation to impact the world. These are the words of Jesus that teach us how to live a happy and productive life.

The psalms are a bit different, however. While the authors of other books tell us about God's plan for us, the psalms are the words of man addressed to God in praise, thanksgiving, supplication, and trust. There are still words of wisdom and instruction, but these are addressed directly to God and we get to "eavesdrop" into the words of praise and adoration. The psalms are the Bible's "choir book." They were sung or chanted to God. We've long lost the hymn tunes, but the words are as powerful as they ever have been.

Generations of us have stood on the shoulders of the psalmists, thinking their thoughts and catching some of their vision. These are words of comfort and strength or guidance and worship. Since none of the Bible was written in English, we are always at the mercy of the interpreter. John Nance Gardner has a good Jewish friend who said to him one day, "John, you had better get me into heaven together with you so that when God speaks to you in Hebrew, I can interpret to you what God is saying!"

Psalm 119 is a beautiful acrostic poem. Each verse begins with the succeeding letters of the Hebrew alphabet, and I'm told that these rhyme. It is composed as praise for God's law. Immediately, we think of the Ten Commandments. These are like the bones of the body. They bring strength and stability to our personal and social lives. Let's hear some of their beauty and wisdom today.

OBSERVATIONS ON THE TEXT

God's laws are merely the framework for our relationships. The law is not static; it is dynamic. God did not stop speaking after he gave the Ten Commandments to Moses. God did not stop speaking after the days of Isaiah and Jeremiah. God did not stop speaking after the words of Jesus or Paul. God is still speaking. The psalmist thinks of the words of God in broad terms of truth from God. These are both rules for how God would have us live and how man hopes God loves and cares for us. Today we are "mining" for jewels from this moving poem. And while we've lost the rhyme, we haven't lost the reason.

There are 70 prayers contained in this psalm. You'll have to dig to find them all or use a Bible commentary. The challenge is not to try to identify all 70 prayers, but to allow some of the prayers in the psalm to speak to you. The psalmist had given a challenge to himself in this writing.

Observations and Opportunities

He was trying to write a series of poetic prayers, with each prayer beginning with the consecutive letters of the Hebrew alphabet—sort of like what we could do with our alphabet:

Amazing is your love, oh God.
Better to be loved by you than to have all the riches of the world.
Convince me, Lord, of the goodness of being your child.
Deliver me from evil and protect me from those who would do me harm.
Establish in me your mind and your heart.
Fill me with your law that I might be the person you would have me to be.

You get the idea. If we had time today, we would write our own psalm of praise in the same way the psalmist did. We might have a little more challenge with Q, X, and Z, but I bet we could come up with a moving set of poetic prayers.

All the commandments are contained within this psalm. The Ten Commandments are not the "Ten Suggestions"! The intention of God is that we live good lives. God knows we will not be perfect. God knows that even when we fall short we will still be loved. Who of us have not had children disappoint us? That doesn't make us love them less; it makes us love them more. The same is true for God, and the psalmist reminds us.

One other point: the law is *not* a substitute for God. The law is not to be worshipped. The law is not a whipping post of unattainable rules. The law is to help us worship God more. The law is to gently guide us into correction. The law is a lamp unto our feet to guide us through the valley of the shadows.

OPPORTUNITIES FOR DAILY LIVING

Over the next few days, read some paragraphs of Psalm 119. The writings are in thoughts of about eight verses each. Read eight verses a day. Meditate on the verses; hear what God might be saying to you. When you identify a benefit or an advantage of the law or a prayer, stop and journal in your own words what God is saying to you.

PRAYER

How good and gracious you are to us, O God. You have given us the bread of life and the living water for the journey ahead. Help us to pay attention to your word, to meditate on it day and night, so that we might dwell with one another in love until we dwell with you in your eternity. Amen.

Intimacy with God
Psalm 139

OPENING

The author of Psalm 139 knew God intimately, and God knew the author intimately. In truth, God knows each of us with a deeper intimacy than we know ourselves. God knows both the good and bad of each of us. God knows the intentions of our hearts, motives that may be buried so far down that we may not even be aware of them.

God's knowledge is unlimited. God's love is universal. God is the creator, owner, judge, and jury of us all. The more we learn about the human body and the natural order of the world, the more we should stand in awe and worship of God.

The writers of the psalms (yes, there were more writers than the shepherd boy David) wrestled with the great issues of life: suffering, sin, death, faith, love, doubt, repentance, joy, praise, lust, hunger—all of the many moods of man. These "songs of praise" are a mirror of our lives. In private devotion and in public worship, they direct our attention to the one who is worthy of our praise and adoration. Let's listen in today to these words of intimate praise from the psalmist.

OBSERVATIONS ON THE TEXT

The psalms were the hymnbook of the early church. Everyone had access to these songs. They hummed them at work, sang them as they traveled, listened to them and sang along in worship. My hunch is that some of the good Jewish worshipers tapped their toes like we do. Just as we sing our favorite hymns, the Jewish people did the same.

Sometimes we glamorize the Bible to the point that we think we are not holy enough to participate. The main point of the Bible is that men of old were no more holy or less holy than we are today. People are people. God knows it; the psalm writers knew it. There are just some of us who try to make the people of the Bible so unattainable that we think we can't ever be as good as them.

Have you read the Bible? Some of the holiest of Bible people did some of the most despicable deeds. The point is that we are not expected to be perfect. But, in Jesus, we can expect to be forgiven!

The Christian discovers the kind of life he should lead or would like to lead and then discovers those lessons in the Bible. The psalms are the hymns of life. I sometimes think that while the Bible is filled with the law, the hymnbook is filled with the ways we should practically live.

Holy Bible, book divine, / Precious treasure, thou art mine;
Mine to tell me whence I came; / Mine to teach me what I am. (John Burton)

Amazing grace! how sweet the sound, / That saved a wretch like me!
I once was lost, but now am found, / Was blind, but now I see. (John Newton)

What a friend we have in Jesus, / All our sins and griefs to bear!
What a privilege to carry / Everything to God in prayer! (Joseph Scriven)

There are many more great hymns we could sing. The hymns are here for us today as they were for the Jews in their day and for so many others who have come before us and will come after us.

Though the created world has lost some of its sacredness to many people, we should still stand in awe of the miracles of creation. We have abandoned the world to the laws of physics, biology, and chemistry. But even in the miracles of scientific discoveries, we need a humble awareness of how the world echoes its creator. After all, who do we think gave all those great scientists their genius? Who do we think gave Einstein his brain? Who do we think gave Churchill his courage? Who do we think brought all of the wonders of science into being? Yes! God!

In beginning to bring order from chaos, God created! Genesis 1 gives us the game plan. God invested his great creative self in this world, in the design of our bodies, in the order of the world. Rather than trying to explain everything away to some scientific law, we should stand in awe and wonder.

How many of us have stood at the bedside of a loved one in critical condition only to see them have a miraculous turnaround and the doctor with a confounded look upon his face? Well, doctor, we know. God hears us when we pray, God sometimes gives us the very desires of our hearts. Science cannot explain the parting of the Red Sea, Jesus walking on water, the raising of Lazarus from the grave, or the resurrection of our Lord. The psalmist wrote songs of faith about the intimacy of God's love and grace. We are fearfully and wonderfully made!

OPPORTUNITIES FOR DAILY LIVING

A child wandering barefoot through the woods is awestruck by the sheer wonder of the environment. He marvels at the psychedelic design of the butterfly. He tries to chase the darting dragonfly. He is breathless as he sees a baby rabbit hopping by.

- Do you remember the innocence of childhood?
- What about our world makes you marvel and breathless today?
- Do you try to explain these happenings away or give glory to God?

We boast that we are *all* created in God's image. Yet many of us try to limit that image to one color or one design. God loves diversity. God lavished color, design, and texture on the world. God gave us the deep black of the African and the brilliant blonde of the Scandinavian. God gave us Italians, Russians, Japanese. God gave us Chinese women who wear pants and men who wear gowns. God gave us hot tea and iced tea. Some cultures begin with dessert while others end with it. We are *all* God's chosen people! The heavens declare his handiwork, and so does mankind.

- Where do you see God's handiwork?
- Do you marvel at God's handiwork or just take it for granted?
- Do you try to embrace diversity or ignore it—or worse?

PRAYER

Search me, O God, and know my heart. Test me and know my thoughts. See if there is any wicked way in me, and lead me in the way everlasting. Amen.

Spying on the promised land
Numbers 13–14

OPENING

There have been those moments when we have experienced the tragedy of making the wrong choice. Every one of us has our tests, which we will meet either with faith and courage or with fear and doubt. Tests will be varied, personal, and challenging. What's most important is the attitude with which we meet these.

By the time of today's lesson, the children of Israel are at Mount Sinai and have been on the road for few years. They are tired, irritable, and ready to settle down into the land of promise God has in store for them. They are on the edge of the fulfillment of their wildest dreams. So God says to Moses, "Send some men to spy out the land and see what's going on over there in Canaan."

The spies return after 40 days with two reports: "We have seen a beautiful land that is overflowing with promise, *but* there is no way we can occupy it." Another man says, "We can take it."

The "safe takers"—those who say we aren't able or that a task cannot be done—are always in the majority. Regardless of the situation, the safe takers are always going to give the "We can't do it!" report. The "risk-takers," always the minority, are those whose faith is secure and whose confidence is high. What is God saying to us today about playing it safe or taking risks?

OBSERVATIONS ON THE TEXT

The strange thing is that, in spite of all the Lord had done for these people, they were willing to take the safe route and ignore taking the land. They wept when they should have been getting ready to move forward. They were silent when they should have been singing. But singing is rarely part of fear. Hugh Thomson Kerr said, "Infidelity never sings; unbelief has no music."

There may be a little bit of the coward in all of us. We all fear something, and it's not always bad to fear. However, after all that God had done, after all the ways God had proved his love and care for these people, they still fell short of faith. It is not a disgrace to be afraid. It is only disgraceful when we surrender to our fears without trying.

The people of Israel committed two sins: complaining of how God was treating them and unbelief that God could take care of them.

The path of faith seems sometimes to cost us as Christians. But how much greater is the ultimate cost of fear? Fear robs us of everything that makes us real people. We fear what people will say, and so we give in to the ways of the world.

Our tests reveal what we are. Do not think that God tests us to find out what we might be made of—God already knows our character. But God wants to reveal to us and to the world around us what we are. We seldom know ourselves as well as we think we do. Caleb passed the test; the others failed. So why did Caleb pass?

For one, he wholly followed the Lord. He was a man fully of God and knew that in God there was nothing good that couldn't be done. We also hear his faith in the report, "If the Lord's delight is in us, rebel not and fear not." Caleb already knew that the Lord delighted in Israel. Israel was on the Lord's side—or rather, the Lord was on their side. Caleb had an active faith, and he was ready to get busy.

Ultimately, only Caleb and Joshua remained steadfast in their faith. Numbers 14:22-24 reports an affirmation from Moses that the nation of Israel was going to follow the report of Caleb.

OPPORTUNITIES FOR DAILY LIVING
- Are you a "safe-keeper" or a "risk-taker"?
- When have you stepped out in faith?
- What keeps you more on the safe side?

The pathway of faith sometimes may seem to cost us way more than we are willing to risk. However, rarely does playing it safe in our faith lead us to the goodness of successful living.

- How are you like the doubting spies?
- How are you like Caleb?
- How does success sustain you?

With every success we find strength and confidence for the next test. We have to look our problems in the face and solve them rather than running from them. Jesus faced harder challenges than we will ever face. We have to claim our faith in Jesus and keep growing in that faith. Success builds success!

- How has the saying that "success builds success" been proven to you?

The passengers on a vessel steaming on the St. Lawrence River became frantic and frightened because of a heavy fog surrounding their boat one evening. In spite of the heavy fog, the captain was maintaining full speed ahead. The mood on the boat became more fearful and even angry. Finally some of the crew said to the passengers, "The fog is low on the water. The captain is high above it and can see where we are going and the way of the river far ahead."

Our captain, too, is far above our fog. God asks that we move forward with him in faith. Fear or faith: the choice is ours. But remember, fear rarely succeeds and faith rarely fails!

PRAYER
Help us to have the faith of Caleb. Help us to see with eyes of faith rather than eyes of fear. Help us to know that, after all you have done for us, you will continue to provide for us. Lord, we believe; help our unbelief! Amen.

Becoming the people of God
Deuteronomy 27–29

OPENING

On Mount Ebal, the tribes of Israel are about to formally become the people of God. This has been quite a journey. Moses and the elders want to be clear about what it means to be God's people. The people have reaffirmed their commitment to God. Now, God is going to be clear about this commitment.

The covenant between God and Israel had long been established in love. But today the nation is about to hear the curses that will come if they disobey. These curses are not meant to scare the nation, but to clarify the expectations of God and to recognize that they would be a just punishment. God wanted the people to understand that there would be consequences if they disobeyed.

God used the process of "call and response" to underscore these consequences. So, all the nation of Israel (and this would have been quite a gathering of men, women, children, cattle, and resources) gathered—a huge encampment. Moses would read the curse, and the people would respond with an "Amen!"

We sometimes have to be reminded of God's expectations of us. Today let us hear the curses, the expectations God has for us. Then let us see how we will respond.

OBSERVATIONS ON THE TEXT

The repetition of many of the curses was to build up picture after picture from different angles for the nation. The hearer is to see, hear, and *never forget* what will happen if disobedience occurs. Moses is appealing to all the senses of the people. This is serious business that they are about to accept. So lengthy is this section on curses (Deut. 27:11-26), that one may well suspect that additions and expansions were added for the purpose of warning the generations to come. These are horrible, serious curses. Perhaps we should take the passing on of our faith as seriously as Moses took his actions on this day.

God and Moses are giving to the children of Israel clear knowledge of what it means to follow God and to be his people. God is saying to Israel, "You are here and I am about to do a huge thing among you." How often has God said this to these people? God is clear: If this is really what you want, here are the rules.

I wonder what would it to do us if we were to hear as clearly the expectations God has for us. I wonder what would happen if we were to hear this passage or passages like the Sermon on the Mount more often than we do. God is always giving us clear messages about his expectations. As Jesus would say, "Let those who have ears hear." We should be paying better attention!

In the chapters that follow, Deuteronomy 28–30, God repeats what has been outlined in chapter 2. The nation is warned to "be careful!" The children of Israel are assured that they know enough if only they will be obedient. The nation is reminded that God is in control of the future; even in the midst of disobedience there will be enduring mercy. The emphasis is on the grace of God in continuing to love and guide the nation. The nation is reminded: "Make no mistake. God is bigger than all of us. God's love is greater than any of us can love, and God's punishment will be worse than any of us want to experience. Live in a spirit of worship, and live in a spirit

Observations and Opportunities

of obedience. God is accessible. God's word is printed on the altar and, even in the midst of the law, there is grace."

Life constantly forces choices upon us. There are political, economic, social, and moral challenges before the nation. When the nation is faced with these challenges, there can be no hesitation. The nation *must choose* obedience or face the consequences. Moses speaks a tender plea to his people: "Choose God!" Make no mistake: God is not taking away man's freedom to make choices; God always gives us this freedom. What God is doing is making very clear the consequences of moral failure.

OPPORTUNITIES FOR DAILY LIVING

Too often we think that consequences when outlined are too harsh. But once again, God is actually giving blessings and freedom. God is saying, "You have the promised land and all the blessings that go with this. Accept me, obey me, and seek me, and all the freedom in the world will be yours. Disobey me and there will be curses to deal with!" That's a loving God and not a punishing God. The boundaries are clear.

Too often as parents we don't do this. Too often we give our children and our children's children too much freedom without explaining to them the consequences. Freedom and consequence are elements of God's love.

- Do you agree that both freedom and consequences are part of God's love? Why or why not?

Formally becoming the people of God is a big deal for Israel. This ceremony represents the ratification of the covenant. God gives the people of Israel the desires of their hearts.

- When has God given you the desires of your hearts?
- What were the circumstances, and how did it feel?
- What did you learn about receiving such a great gift from God?

As each curse and expectation was read, Israel was required to respond with a resounding "Amen!" We have lost much of the power of this word in the modern age. When an "Amen" was given in Old Testament days, this was a solemn oath. The people of Israel were saying, "Assuredly, sincerely, deep in our souls, we agree to this!" We should be as careful today with our "amen" responses.

The most steadying, affirming, guiding influence in our lives is our relationship to God. We should say a resounding "Amen!" from the depths of our souls. But we know people who have given lip service to this. We have to pay attention. Those who are disobedient to the covenant are still at risk of God's curses. Our only promise of protection is Jesus, the new covenant of God's grace.

PRAYER

Amen, O God! We have heard the expectations you have for us. We have heard the curses you have set before us. We also know that our only hope for glory is in Jesus the Christ. Help us to receive Jesus as our own and to share Jesus so that all may know. Amen.

A good woman*
Proverbs 31

OPENING

Proverbs 30:11-14 identifies four types of evil persons: those who openly defy or dishonor parents, the self-righteous, the proud, and those who exploit others. Respect for parents is the mark of a wise and righteous person. The foundation of society is built upon those who care for the aging. There are those who think they are better than anyone else. They think they have never sinned; in fact, they think they have never had a bad thought. Pride prevents us from growing; pride produces instability, fear, and contention; and pride insults God. There are those who take unfair advantage of others, who use people for their own selfish outcomes. These too are an affront to God. We are not objects; we are part of God's created order.

What can keep us from these four types of evil? I would tell you that a strong woman—a good wife and good mother—can do this. The mother of King Lemuel in Proverbs 31 would agree. Now you men may think that you are the leaders in today's world—and many of you are. But let me remind you that most of you were formed by strong Christian mothers and grandmothers who made sure you obeyed the commands of the Lord.

Proverbs 31 extols the virtues of women. These words may make some of you men squirm. Good! We need to hear these words today.

OBSERVATIONS ON THE TEXT

The first nine verses of this chapter contain the admonitions of a mother to her son who is the king. This unknown king and his unknown mother give good advice about leadership. No son of mine, no son of my womb and, more importantly, nor my vows, will give in to the things that will destroy his leadership—not strong drink, the perversion of the rights of the poor, ignoring poverty and misery, being distracted by women. These destroy; they do not build up. Men, you must stay on your guard. Your momma is there to help you learn these lessons, but it is up to you to pay attention to the lessons she has taught you. Too many men have seen their downfall because they have forgotten the God-given lessons passed down by their Christian parents, especially their mothers.

Verses 10-31 then shift to talk about the good woman. This is an acrostic poem using every letter of the Hebrew alphabet to talk about the goodness of a woman. This could be interpreted in our day as "Here is the ideal woman from A to Z!" Women are important, more so now perhaps than at any other time in human history. Yes, Columbus discovered America, but Isabella financed the trip from her palace household money!

And if it hadn't been for women, we might not be here in Houston. There have been daring women since the first defiant bite that Eve took in the Garden. Women are innovative. Women are sometimes put in a bad light in Scripture. Of course, we think the Bible was written by men! But I am grateful for this passage and others in Scripture that remind us that both men and women can be godly and ungodly. Remember, in biblical days a woman was little more than a possession like a good horse or cow. Women were to bear children, preferably male offspring. If they didn't produce male babies, if they did the laundry wrong, or if they burned the biscuits, they could be put out on the street! Not a very good place to be.

As we read Proverbs 31, however, we get a different perspective. And, while the writer of this chapter is relating specifically to the ideal "wife," the implication is that it is the same for the ideal woman. The ideal woman has found the secrets of worthwhile living and has passed this on to her daughters and their daughters. How important the teachings of my mother and grandmother have been to me! While men could do all manner of evil and "get away with it," the women were expected to be upright and godly. Women have always been at the center of Christian piety.

OPPORTUNITIES FOR DAILY LIVING

Husbands are to respect and honor their wives and to treat them better than mere property. (Jesus would echo these words when he came on the scene.) Women are not to be embarrassed, but encouraged and honored. Women are to be recognized for their achievements and given reasons to be loved and secure. Women are to be given reasons to laugh and to enjoy life.

Why is a good woman such a rare find? The writer of these verses explains in detail. And, while we will not find any one woman who practices literally every aspect described in this passage, we aspire to these high standards as women (and you men should encourage us).

A good woman is dependable and trustworthy, loyal and supportive, industrious and willing, hardworking and persistent. A good woman is not weak and helpless and is prepared to show quality and good taste. A good woman promotes her husband's reputation and develops the talents of her children. A good woman is a kind and wise teacher, a good manager, deserves respect, and has a strength of piety.

Above all, as the Book of Proverbs ends, the sign of a good woman is that her children rise up and call her blessed and her husband praises her. And while women have done excellent things, they are still not superior to God. The good woman honors the Lord, praises God for God's goodness, and her works are praised throughout the city.

PRAYER

Thank you, God, for the wonderful women in our lives. Thank you for the godly women in our class and in our church. Thank you for those special women in our world who have made a difference in our society. Help us to be responsible in the goodness and blessings you have given us that we might continue to raise up the generations to come to honor and bless your holy name. Amen.

*Eula Mae wrote this lesson sometime in the early 1960s. Her writing and margin notes indicate that, once again, she was ahead of her time!

Citizens of two nations
Amos 4, 5

OPENING

The typical American's day begins when he gets out of bed in his pajamas—a garment of East Indian origin. He drinks his coffee grown from an Abyssinian plant—first discovered by Arabs. If it looks like rain, he puts on rubber shoes—of ancient Mexican origin. He might use his umbrella—invented in India. He might sprint for the train—invented by the British. He reads the news imprinted with characters—invented by ancient Semites. The news is printed by a process—invented in Germany. His paper is printed in ink—invented in China. If he reads bad news, he is thankful to God—by way of a religion passed on from ancient Hebrews. Yep, this man is 100 percent American, and he is very thankful to be so.

Citizenship has not always come easily. In the time of Caesar the best and brightest of Rome were awarded citizenship, but not so the common people. Some soldiers were awarded citizenship upon their retirement (or death) from the military. Some Roman rulers sold citizenships to those who could afford it (see Acts 22:27-29). Finally, in 212 AD, citizenship was granted to all free persons of the empire.

To be a citizen of any country means that we submit to a discipline that makes absolute demands upon our loyalty and devotion. There is also the vertical dimension that must be considered. We owe our nation a debt. Yet, national pride and patriotism should *never* conflict with the allegiance we have to God. In 1776 Benjamin Franklin served with a group of patriots charged with developing the national seal. Franklin wanted the back side of the seal to depict Moses crossing the Red Sea and the hand of God striking Pharaoh with overflowing waters. Franklin wanted the inscription on the seal to read: "Rebellion to Tyrants is Obedience to God."

Throughout American history, even during modern-day history, God has been at the center of the lives of presidents, generals, and congressmen. However, we may see shifts away from our faith.

Are you aware of any warnings we in America have today that might be God-sent? Are you paying attention to the decline of allegiance to God in our nation? Do you feel any personal responsibility? Let us continue to pray that our nation will claim God at the center of our lives.

OBSERVATIONS ON THE TEXT

In today's lesson, Israel is turning away from God. Amos is calling the nation back to the simplicity of a deep and abiding faith in God. The wealthy are gaining even more wealth at the expense of the poor. Injustices and immoralities hold the day. The wealthy continue to bring ostentatious tithes and sacrifices—not for forgiveness or to please God, but so they can keep on sinning with a clear conscience. Amos calls the rich "cows of Bashan." This is *not* a compliment! Amos makes it clear that the God of all holiness will not close his eyes to this bad behavior. The children of Israel have lost their way and are once again not paying attention to their need for God.

A nation and its citizens will reap what they sow. God tells Israel: "After all I have done for you, your privilege and status, you are not exempt. You are not immune from my punishment." God is a just God and does not tolerate spoiled children. Not one of us can escape God's punishment when we misbehave. Not one of us will get a free pass from God's corrective action.

Many Americans have assumed that we are now the elect. We may talk about being God's elect, but we are fools if we think we can get by without feeling the effects of our moral failings. Violent and major crimes are on the rise in our nation. Murder is fast becoming our number-one problem. Alcoholism is our number-one social problem and the number-three reason for death in our country. We have glamorized sex to the point of producing illegitimate children. We see the rising rate of abortions and the growing rate of divorce. Everything is deemed acceptable and, if you speak out against anything, you are dismissed with the words, "Don't be so old-fashioned!"

We Christians have got to do something. Yet, most of us are not even aware of the problems facing our nation. In America we still have freedom. We have the freedom to express our worries in speech and in writing. We can write to our elected officials and political leaders about our concerns.* There still are enough real Christians to counteract negative influences and to keep our ideals high and noble. We must stay true to our witness and instruct those in our homes and workplaces in words and actions. And, we must remember that in America we too are under God's sovereign power. All nations are under God!

OPPORTUNITIES FOR DAILY LIVING

The history of the world is filled with arrogant nationalists. This does not mean we should not be loyal to our nation and proud of our nation. However, our patriotism ends when our national policies and actions are contrary to God's commands. We have to speak out when we see injustices. We have to act according to our Christian witness to stand up for the poor and the abused. Words without actions are meaningless. I am an American and proud to be so. But I am first and foremost a Christian. Yes, my prayer continues to be, "God bless America, land that I love." And, my prayer is also, "God keep us right; but when we are wrong, make us right!"

- How aware are you of the problems in our nation?
- What are you willing to do as a Christian and as a citizen to make our nation right?

We have a moral obligation as Christians to use our words for correction. Speak out. When appropriate, write letters to political leaders. Use the power of your Christian witness both in word and action in your workplace, in your home, and in your social interactions.

- How bold are you in your Christian witness?
- How willing are you to say, "Rebellion to tyrants is obedience to God"?

PRAYER

God, bless us as citizens of your reign and of our nation. Help us to love you and love our neighbors. Let our witness keep us faithful while sharing your love with a world that needs your wisdom and guidance. Thank you for our freedom, our ultimate freedom in Jesus, our Christ. Amen.

Eula Mae's files contain a copy of a letter she sent to the U.S. Supreme Court. Stapled to the copy are the names of the then-sitting justices, with checkmarks indicating she had mailed a copy to each of them.

The gift of faithfulness
Matthew 1

OPENING

My favorite words from our Singing Christmas Tree production are from this song: "There in a stable, the Father's only son, chose to give Himself through human birth. And when the cry of a baby pieced the universe, once for all, all men were shown their worth."

How deeply God must love you and me. Was that first Christmas necessary to make the Kingdom of God possible for us?

Matthew's Christmas story is not about Mary or Joseph or the star or the wise men. Matthew's story is about Jesus. For Matthew, Jesus is not an extension of God but the fulfillment of God.

Jesus is unique in origin, in character, and in function. Of all the names given to Jesus, perhaps the most meaningful one to me is "Emmanuel," which translates "God with us." God is with me, right here, right now for always. And that is indeed a wonderful Christmas gift.

OBSERVATIONS ON THE TEXT

If you were to select three qualities for an ideal husband or an ideal wife, what would they be? Well, God must have selected Joseph and Mary very carefully. They were surely a match made in heaven.

When we have been hurt, our first reaction is to hurt back. Joseph had every reason to humiliate Mary for she had surely humiliated him. And the best she could offer was "God did this to me!" Who among us would have believed such a story?

But, the Bible tells us that Joseph was a righteous man and not willing to put her to shame. These seem to be complimentary terms, but actually they are contrasts. A "righteous" man could not continue in a relationship with a woman who appeared to be an adulteress. He could have broken their relationship; he could have publicly shamed her; he could have even had her put to death by stoning. His head may have told him to remove her from his life.

But his heart was filled with love! You see, deep hurt in a relationship is not the opposite of love. Hurt means the deeper dimension of love. Joseph loved Mary with all his heart. He did not want to disgrace her; he did not want to lose her love. He was not flippant about his predicament. He prayed about what he should do. But being righteous and just, he stood with his betrothed and claimed her as his wife and proclaimed his love for her. This was truly a remarkable man who stood behind her in the manger that first Christmas. We need more men like Joseph.

Would you believe an angel? Would you even recognize an angel? Well, Joseph did. Three times angels spoke to Joseph, and each time he paid attention. Joseph had an openness to incredible possibilities. He didn't limit God. He didn't say, "I won't obey." He lived faithfully into the goodness of God.

After working thru his hurt, Joseph made adjustments and got Mary out of town. He knew wagging tongues would be hard at work. So, he took her with him to Bethlehem. Besides being a faithful man, he was a compassionate and loving husband. He was sensitive to the leading of God. He was a man of faith, of obedience, and love.

Observations and Opportunities

God purposefully put Jesus under the influence of this good man. Joseph was not the star of the Jesus play, but he played his part to the fullest and brought up the earthly Jesus in the fear and admonition and love of God. Perhaps for us, too, when the curtain comes down on our earthly drama we have been found faithful—playing our parts just right!

So, what about the wise men in Matthew 2? These Persian, Gentile men were recognized teachers of religion and science of their day. They came prepared to worship and pay homage to this holy family. They didn't come to gawk or satisfy their curiosity, but in reverence and wonder and awe.

How did the wise men know about the birth of Jesus? They were paying attention! They knew more than all the advisors of Herod. And, these wise men came bearing gifts. But they didn't bring gifts to Herod. They came into the mouth of evil and were wise enough to know what to share and what not to share. They were wise on how to travel. They were wise enough to pay attention to God and not to the king. And, when they found the manger, they were overcome with joy. That's when the gifts were given. It's amazing how joy elicits gifts and evil drives them away!

OPPORTUNITIES FOR DAILY LIVING

Joseph was a good man of faith, obedience, and love. He taught his son with intentionality. He framed his son in the spirituality of that which brought him into this world. Joseph taught Jesus not only how to be a godly man, but also how to relate redemptively with others. No wonder that years later Jesus, who was nurtured by this good earthly father, would say to a fallen woman: "I do not condemn you! Get up and go about your business and sin no more!"

- Who taught you how to be a person of faith?
- Who are some people who have hurt you who need your forgiveness?
- How can you, like Mary and Joseph, help develop good Christian families?
- Have you ever seen an angel? If so, how did you know?

What do angels do in our world? What did angels do in the time of Jesus? I believe there are angels among us. I know that some of you are angels! You are the best friends and the best Christmas present I know.

- What will we do with our gifts for our class, for our church, for our world?
- What makes a person wise?
- How did Jesus' visitors from the East know whom to trust?
- How did they know the trickery of Herod?
- How do we know the trickery of those around us who would lead us into evil?
- What gifts do we have for Jesus this year?

PRAYER

Merry Christmas, God. Thank you for the goodness of Joseph and Mary. Thank you for the wisdom of the wise men. Thank you for the angelic messengers who kept Joseph and Mary faithful. And most of all, thank you for the love that became Jesus—the greatest gift of all time!

The gift of availability
Luke 2

OPENING

Luke 2 begins with Caesar Augustus. Just who was this man? At the time he was probably the most powerful man on earth, the emperor of Rome. He was the great nephew of Julius Caesar and adopted by Julius Caesar as his son and heir. He stood in an obvious dangerous position after the assassination of Julius.

However, Augustus steadily won his way to power against Mark Antony and other rivals until at last he was seated on the imperial throne and given the new name of Augustus by the Roman senate. Rome extended all over the known world from Britain to Asia. The census of Luke 2 is that *all* the world should be taxed. This would have been a huge undertaking. The very name of Rome meant wealth, power, and authority. Augustus ruled from 27 BC to 14 AD.

Israel was a little speck on the map of the empire. No one cared what happened in this insignificant part of the great Roman Empire. Caesar Augustus could have cared less. The Roman senate and the rest of the empire could have cared less. Israel was not the "middle of nowhere"—it was way out past the middle of nowhere, as far as Rome was concerned.

And, in this little insignificant area of the world, God chose to perform the most significant event in the history of the world. We have a God who knows how to live life to the fullest. God wants the best for us. And into a world where Rome thought itself bigger than God, God chose an insignificant little town to become the center of the world. About 700 years prior to the first Christmas, Isaiah had predicted that this event would happen. But Rome in her arrogance never paid attention to the "little" prophets in Israel. And, Rome also ignored the fact that Israel bore the title of "God's chosen people." So, here comes Jesus.

OBSERVATIONS ON THE TEXT

Joseph and Mary loaded up the donkey and made the trip from Nazareth to Bethlehem to register. Now, typically the women stayed home. The men made the trip to get registered. But Mary was in a tough spot, great with child and unmarried. And Joseph was in a tough spot because he didn't know what to do with this woman who could only say "I'm pregnant because the Holy Spirit covered me." So, Joseph being a good man, a forgiving man, and in love with Mary regardless of her condition, took her with him to Bethlehem. This got Mary out of town and away from the pain of gossip. This allowed Mary and Joseph to do some bonding as they traveled. Perhaps this allowed some of the stress of their relationship to ease.

Rarely in a marriage is everything perfect, good, and calm. There is always something out of whack, causing some stress, challenging the strength and depth of the love of the marriage. Joseph and Mary had more than their fair share. But Joseph and Mary had both been affirmed by God of this happenstance. And both of them were faithful and trusting in God.

If the innkeeper had only known that the Savior of the world was to be born at his place, he would have rearranged his guests! But the "Holiday Inn" was full, and the innkeeper had no idea what was about to happen. We never know when the great possibilities of God are at our door *unless* we keep our hearts open and our spirits sensitive to his leadership.

How often do we see an ordinary stranger and ignore them because we have no more room in our lives for another person? How many times have we not built friendships with extraordinary people because we just had no more time or energy for building another friendship?

And so, Mary and Joseph stayed "out back in the barn" and tried to get as comfortable as possible. And, wouldn't you know it? This is the time that God chose for Jesus to be born. Jesus came into the world, not just in an insignificant part of the world but in an insignificant part of town. Wouldn't it have been funny if years later Joseph had said, "Boy close the door to the house. You think you were born in a barn?" Really, it wasn't even a barn. It was a crèche or a stable. We call it a manger, just a place to tie up the animals for the night, not to keep them out of the weather. This was the birthplace for the Son of God.

In verses 8-11 the angels appear to the shepherds. They come with a great message for the whole world. This is a pivotal event in history: the calendar would be changed even for atheists. The angels' appearance would have been sensational! God is always sensational, even in the seemingly insignificant times and places. Think about some of God's sensational acts. The angel of the Lord or the heavenly host or the angel choir is always present as God is working. The birth of Jesus involved all the angels of heaven singing.

In verses 8-20 we see the shepherds interacting with the angels. Why didn't the angels appear to the Roman senate or directly to Caesar Augustus? Why didn't God choose to appear to the elite of the community at least?

The shepherds were the most insignificant people in the community. They were the lowliest of the lowly. Sometimes those who have very little are the most receptive, most appreciative, even the most obedient persons.

The shepherds feared, they listened, and they ran quickly to see. And they returned as transformed men. They may still have had no standing in the community, but they now knew that God was not distant; that God was near; that they had beheld God's son in the flesh. From now on they would be different.

OPPORTUNITIES FOR DAILY LIVING

What God can do with Mary, Joseph, and the shepherds, God can do with us! Are you willing to endure shame and pain to be used of God? On those days when you feel insignificant, can you remember that you are important to God, an instrument of peace, a witness to the King of Glory?

The angels sang with glory! Mary sang with thanksgiving! In the midst of stress and trouble, we need to be reminded to sing praises to God. In the midst of our depression or sadness, we should sing.

- How do you sing?
- What is your favorite Christmas carol? Why?
- What is the deeper meaning of the carol that brings hope and affirmation to you?

PRAYER

Happy Birthday, Jesus. Thank you so much for giving us the best present ever: the hope of glory. Help us to pay attention to the mighty works of God. Help us to pay attention to your presence in the world. Help us to be your disciples. Amen.

The gifts of the wise men*
Matthew 2:1-12

OPENING

Yes, it is true: It is the thought that counts. And as we look at these beautifully wrapped packages around us today, we know that some deep, personal thought has gone into each of these gifts. There are some great gifts in these boxes. Are you excited to see them?

Now the wise men of Matthew 2 brought some great gifts with them to honor Jesus. We are told that they brought gold, frankincense, and myrrh. These would have been amazing gifts. These would surely have implied that deep thought had gone into what they were bringing to the Baby Jesus and his family. And we could all probably give gifts of this extravagance to our church. Is this really what the Christ child expects from us?

So, I'm going to unwrap these gifts today. These are the gifts from the modern-day wise men and wise women. We can choose to share them with Jesus or not! But, I want you to consider what you might can give.

(Eula Mae then unwraps each gift and pulls out sheets of paper with words written on them.)

The first gift we should give Jesus is CONCERN.

There are hungry, sick, cold, disappointed, and disillusioned people all around us. Most importantly, there are people around us who do not know Jesus. From those at our front door, the homeless mission, a bit further away at Round Rock (Texas) where the crops are drying up and the town is dying, people need us to be concerned for them. Jesus needs us to be concerned for them. We need to give the gift of sincere concern and compassion in the same way that Jesus did: "When he saw the crowds, he had compassion for them, because they were harassed and helpless, like sheep without a shepherd" (Matt. 9:3).

Another gift we should give Jesus is CONSCIOUS WITNESS.

The spoken word, shared in the right way, to the right person, at the right time is very powerful. This is a deliberate planned action that takes our arrogance out of the equation and shares an intimate invitation to accept Christ. We underestimate the abilities Christ has given us. We underestimate the power of a personal invitation. The people in our life who we see daily . . . many of these are not Christians and need the love of Jesus. The people we see on the streets . . . many of these are not Christians and need the love of Jesus. We cannot leave the evangelism of the world just to the missionaries that we send money to. Other religions are being much more aggressive than we are. In East Pakistan there are 44,000,000 people but only 50,000 are Christians. Let it be said of us that we are doing all we can for the Kingdom of God!

INFLUENCE is the next gift we can give to Jesus.

Influence is our unconscious witness. This is the result of my attitudes, my daily habits, my Sunday habits, my casual conversations. These are those serendipity moments when God puts in front of us opportunities to use our influence for his glory.

In the Gaza/Egypt area, in the midst of the desert, we have a Baptist hospital. On clinic days the beautiful compound is covered in carefully watered grass with a few shade trees. And this grass is so covered with people who need help that you cannot see a single blade of grass. Many have walked all night to get to the hospital. When the main doctor of the hospital walks by, many people quickly stand and give him a salute—for they all love him. He has tended to them, to their family members, and to their loved ones for years. He lives among them, and he loves them.

A 14-year-old boy says of the doctor: "There is something different about the hospital and the people who work here. The doctor loves me. He loves all of us. He makes us feel good. And no matter how sick we are, he cares."

This oasis in the desert is drawing people to Christ through its gracious Christian influence. It shares a conscious witness of Christ through the excellent medical care it gives. It also shares an unconscious witness of Christ through the love and personal relationships the staff shares. This hospital is changing the world for Christ.

Eula Mae unwraps a smaller box and pulls out a $100 bill.

My MONEY represents my energy, my commitment, my influence, my very being. It is here that our desire to be faithful is really tested. We have worked hard for our money. Many of us are asked to give to so many good causes. Many of us suffer from what is called "donor fatigue" by sociologists. John and I choose to give our money to good Christian causes. My money, our money is how we help our church grow. Our money is how we support mission efforts like that hospital around the world.

Money that we give helps print Bibles through a Baptist publishing house in Rio. Our money helped build a church building in Costa Rica. Our money helps support a Hungarian refugee here in our community and helps educate a young Korean girl in South Korea.

Now, John and I don't accomplish this by ourselves. We give our money, and it combines with your money, and then that money combines with other people's money, and together we have the resources to change the world. We call this the Cooperative Program, where Baptists around the world all give and cooperatively share in the needy places. But it starts with my check going to my church and then going around the world for the cause of Christ.

PRAYER is the final gift that modern-day wise men and wise women can give.

There is so little time to pray and so much to pray about. As I count my blessings, prayers of praise, thanksgiving and adoration, I pray with such gratitude.

My intercessory prayers include unknown people, missionaries around the world, pastors of our church, and so many others. I pray for our church. I pray for each of you. I pray that God will intercede and use all of us to make a difference in the world, and that all with know the name of Jesus and be saved.

There are so many more gifts we can give to our Jesus. These are just a few. My prayer today is that you will choose one or more or even all of these and share enthusiastically. Because as we know, it is the thought that counts. But, it is the giving and doing that really matters! Amen.

*Eula Mae did not write this lesson in her typical format. On this Christmas day she presented a dramatic monologue on the gifts of the wise men as if 1962 was the first Christmas. She had wrapped boxes in bright paper and brought these into the classroom—perhaps even a few weeks prior to Christmas to create some interest. This is just one more indication of Eula Mae's depth of understanding for teaching adults.

Happy Christians
Matthew 5:1-15

OPENING

The happy Christian is an influential Christian. Today we hear Jesus bringing words of the Kingdom of God: happiness, influence, and righteousness. Jesus gives us blessings that no one else can give. We are blessed when we are poor in spirit, when we are meek, when we are hungry, when we are persecuted for the sake of Jesus. We are blessed when we mourn, and we will be comforted. Life is not given for our comfort only; we also share in our neighbors' pain and comfort. Life, according to Jesus, is not a problem to be solved but a grand adventure of goodwill to be undertaken.

For Jesus, the plight of "man" was worth paying attention to. In the Beatitudes, Jesus touches all of us in some way and gives us blessings that make life worth living. Who among us has not been poor in spirit, or mourned, or been hungry for God's righteousness? No matter where we find ourselves, Jesus says that blessings are "a' comin!" What helps you embrace happiness? What blessings would you like today from Jesus?

OBSERVATIONS ON THE TEXT

The Beatitudes deal with opposites. If you are poor in spirit, you will become proud in spirit. If are meek, you will find mental strength. Jesus knew that all of us, at our cores, hunger and thirst for righteousness. Our souls long for completeness. Every hunger and thirst has its answer: food and drink. Righteousness plus equity lead to a justice held in love that fulfills our hunger and thirst.

Some hungers when fulfilled are mocked. Some people long for praise and adulation, but when they receive these, they find them to be empty. So, this need becomes like a drug leading to more and more acting-out. The soul does not find satisfaction in empty praise. Some people long for riches, which are found to be empty. Some long for power; which is also empty. Some long for fame and fortune, which are also empty. The soul at its core is only complete and the hunger and thirst only satisfied in the blessings of Jesus.

Some hungers when fulfilled lead us to higher hungers. Once our basic needs are met in Jesus, we then begin to hunger for the right things. We hunger for the higher longing for love and find it fulfilling. We hunger for beauty and, when we see it, are fulfilled. We hunger for music and find ourselves tapping our feet or singing out loud. We hunger for truth, hoping that Jesus will also fulfill this.

The strength of the blessing is in the goodness. Goodness always overcomes evil. What goodness can do to evil is greater than what evil can do to goodness. So, be happy. The happy Christian is an influential Christian. There is so much good that we can do in our world. As happy Christians, there is no limit to the influence we can have on government, on poverty, on race relations, on religion, on business. As Christians, we are no good unless we are having a positive influence on the world for Jesus.

The second half of the Beatitudes continues the thought of influence. What is the implication of a happy Christian? We use our influence for salt and light in the world. The candle itself is not the influencer; a candle is useless without its flame. The *flame* is the influencer. Salt is not the influencer, but alone is just something to be trampled on. The *flavor* that salt adds to food is the influencer. We are not the influencers unless our good works are pointing to the glory of God. Some of us have work to do. My life is still a work in progress. What about yours?

OPPORTUNITIES FOR DAILY LIVING

Life, according to Jesus, is not a problem to be solved but a grand adventure of goodwill to be undertaken. The living of a good life should be a dominant hunger. As we accept the happiness Jesus gives us, we begin to hunger for deeper urges such as seeking beauty, love, and truth.

- What hungers have you had for which the fulfillment continues to leave you empty?
- What does this emptiness tell you?
- What hungers are you feeling in your life today?
- How can Jesus satisfy you with blessings?

We are to be influencers. If we are happy in Jesus, we can be influencers for Jesus.

- Where are you using your influence for the Kingdom of God?
- Where are you using your influence to make our world a better place?
- How can you do more to use your influence?
- Are you more salt or light? Why?
- How are you bringing light to the world?
- How are you adding flavor to the world?
- How do you know when you've "arrived"?

My life is still a work in progress. John and I pray daily for our continued close walk with Jesus and with each other.

PRAYER

Thank you, God, for the blessings of my life. Help me to continue to hunger and thirst for your righteousness. Help me to continue to seek the higher ideals of beauty, truth, justice, and peace. Help me to be light and salt in our world—to use my influence for your will. Amen!

Keeping the law
Matthew 5:27-37

OPENING

A wealthy businessman bragged to his pastor about his plans to visit the Holy Land. "And while I'm there, I'm going to read the Ten Commandments aloud from the top of Mt. Sinai!" Unimpressed, the minister commented, "Perhaps a better plan would be to stay at home and keep them!"

Today we are looking at Jesus and his relationship to the law. A free society cannot exist without a moral base. Christianity is not a set of rigid rules but a standard for living life in love. So today we will set aside our biases and perhaps hear a new word from Jesus.

OBSERVATIONS ON THE TEXT

We all have an "outer" world that is public. We all have an "innerr" world that is private. We are aware of our outer world because that is what people judge us by. But the inner world is even more important. It is our *character*. What we do is never more important than who we are. We cannot let our work, our relationships, our politics, or anything else get in the way of who we are and how we relate to others.

Jesus stringently objected to the scribal law. The scribes had made the law a joke. They had defined everything according to petty rules. The Sabbath rules were the most petty of all.

Food equaled a bite of a dried fig. Drinking milk was limited to one swallow. Drinking water was limited to the amount used to swab an eye. Using ink was limited to only enough to write two letters of the alphabet. The scribes spent endless hours arguing whether a man could move a candle from one place in the house to another or whether a tailor sinned if he went out with a needle in his robe.

Jesus did not want to do away with the law, but he saw it as the minimum standard—not the ultimate. When Jesus said he came to fulfill the law, he meant to bring out the real meaning of the law. Behind the law was one great principle: A man must seek God's will and, when he discovers it, he must dedicate his whole life to obeying God's will.

Jesus dedicated his ministry to leading people to respect others and to have reverence for God. We are to respect our parents, our friends, our lives, our property. We are to have reverence for God, for God's name, for God's holy day. We are to master our needs and respect ourselves so that our wrong desires may never master us.

The scribes and Pharisees lived under the motive of the law. They lived to satisfy the demands of the law. The Christian, on the other hand, is to live by the motive of *love*. The law is limited, but love goes on eternally; love is not limited.

Five times in this chapter we read that Jesus said, "You have heard it said, but I tell you. . ."

Why is anger wrong? Why are lust and adultery wrong? Why is divorce wrong? Why are false oaths wrong? All of these are about wanting something we have no right to have.

David lusted after Bathsheba. David had plenty of women, plenty of money, plenty of fame. But he didn't have Bathsheba. He took her anyway; he sinned. Jesus said that adultery is not only a forbidden act but also a forbidden thought (lust). And Jesus went on to say that anything that lures a man to his own ruin must be done away with. Jesus started naming body parts that might cause adultery and lust, and he suggested these just be cut off! Perhaps he was exaggerating for effect, but he sure got the men's attention! Jesus gave two suggestions:

Quit thinking the thoughts that cause you to stumble. The cure for evil thinking is good action. This applies to men and women.

Fill your mind with "Peter Pan" thoughts: "Just think wonderful lovely thoughts, and they will lift you up in the air!"

Christianity had two audiences early on: the Jews and the Romans/Greeks. For both of these male audiences, a wife was simply property with no say to life. She could be divorced just because she displeased her husband. (He didn't even need a lawyer!) Women had no social standing or rights. Respectable women were isolated and were around only for bearing legitimate heirs (more males). The ancient world would have been shocked to learn of the demands made today of Christian chastity!

In our world today, affairs still happen. Usually the couple has already allowed the marriage to die. The cure for divorce is to rekindle the flame of love between a husband and wife. Spending less time on things and more time on each other will make love last.

OPPORTUNITIES FOR DAILY LIVING

Keeping our minds on what is most important keeps us from trivializing life.

- What shape is your "outer" world in?
- What shape is your "inner" world in?
- What are you doing to build a happy marriage, healthy emotions, and honest language?

When Sysco was thinking of dividing shares of stock, Herb Liebich said, "We all trust John Baugh. I move we accept his evaluations without even opening them!" (This was based on years of dealing with John!) Your reputation matters!

- What are you doing to keep your reputation strong, your word trustworthy?
- Where are you spending your time that is taking you away from your family?

Perhaps you need a second honeymoon. Maybe you need a weekly date night. Maybe you need to have a courtship again. Ask God where you are lacking in your marriage and family relationships, and then do something to strengthen these.

PRAYER

Lord, help me to live right. Help me to keep my heart in tune with you. Help me to treat people with respect and to treat you with reverence. Help me, O God, to seek your will and not my own. Amen.

Prayer and priorities
Matthew 6:1-18

OPENING

At the recent funeral of a pillar of the church, the pastor gave a listing of all this man had accomplished. When hearing of the spiritual accomplishments of someone, are you inspired or intimidated? Why?

Today we encounter Jesus' thoughts on prayer and priorities. Prayer is not a beggar sitting on a mat; prayer is friendship with the Great Companion. In prayer we share our thoughts, feelings, and needs with God. And we open ourselves up to receive what God has in store for us.

Is prayer just selfish petition? No! Prayer is a way of being honest about our own needs and open to God's responding.

OBSERVATIONS ON THE TEXT

Fasting: Fasting is a show to God of our sincerity and focus. Christian discipline should be positive, radiant, and humble. Fasting is a preparation for bearing fruit. Fasting helps us focus on the right priorities.

Focus: Jesus gave us a positive, active admonition for defeating worry. Seek first the Kingdom of God, not your own kingdom. Concentrate on doing God's will. The rule and reign of God in our lives is God's love, loving God and loving one another. When we are motivated by love in all we do, we are right on target in our prayers and in our daily living.

All the pronouns in the Lord's Prayer are plural. We don't pray "my Father"—we pray *our* Father, *our* daily bread, *our* trespasses. Jesus was concerned that his followers have the right focus. Jesus wanted us to pay attention to God's will and God's love. Jesus wanted us to pay attention to one another. Jesus did not come to develop selfish, self-centered followers.

The novelist Alexandre Black was fond of asking, "If you were to receive one million dollars today, what would you do with it?" This was his way of learning of another's priorities.

What are your priorities? How would one million dollars change your life?

Jesus knew that his followers would do religious acts and do the right things. What he wanted for them was pure motives without the showiness of the Pharisees. Jesus advised his followers: When tempted to show it, hide it. When tempted to hide it, show it.

Reward: Everyone usually gets what they seek. If we want payment in full, we get paid. If we want to be noticed by others, we get noticed. If we want to worry, we worry. If we store up treasures on earth, we have our reward. Instead, we must seek what God wants for us. What we give top priority to reveals our true love.

The Kingdom of God is what we seek. And as we seek, God keeps us. We must constantly and consistently submit ourselves to God. Isaiah 26:3 tells us, "Those of steadfast mind, you keep in peace—in peace because they trust in you."

Hypocrites: Originally the word hypocrite meant "play acting." Then it came to mean one who pretended to be something he was not. We are not to call attention to our good deeds. We are called to humility. The Pharisees made a point of giving their offerings at the busiest time of the day. They made a great show of their gifts. But Jesus knew for whom these acts were performed.

The lilies of the field show us how to act with humility. These flowers receive naturally, staying receptive to the world around them—the rain, the sun, the soil. They receive from God what God intended until they bloom beautifully. They don't play act. They don't pretend to be something they are not. They don't call attention to their blooms.

OPPORTUNITIES FOR DAILY LIVING

Tauler, a German mystic, wrote one day about his encounter with a beggar. The beggar said to him, "When my day is good, I thank God. When it rains, I thank God. When I am hungry, I thank God. I thank God and, since God's will is my will, whatever pleases God pleases me. Why should I be unhappy when I am not?"

We should all learn to live in the happiness of God's love and guidance for us. Mostly we talk about our concerns, but this is merely a pretense and not true generosity.

- Do your checkbook and personal calendar reflect your concern for the less fortunate?
- If you were to receive a million dollars, how would you help those who are less fortunate?

A little girl was on her first train ride. The weather was not good, the train was rocking back and forth, and darkness was approaching as the train entered a treacherous mountain pass. The little girl remained calm. A nervous passenger looked at the calm little girl and asked, "Aren't you worried about the train going off the tracks?" The little girl replied, "No sir. My father is the engineer!"

And so it is with us! Every day is a good day; our heavenly father is driving the train.

PRAYER

O God, forgive us when we are filled with worry, anxiety, and selfishness. Help us, Lord, to focus all our life on you and all that you provide. Help us to truly seek you first. Amen.

Don't worry about worry
Matthew 6:24-34

OPENING

There is no one on earth who worries like I do. I have joined the new "Don't Worry Club." And now I hold my breath and worry that I'm not worrying. Worry is so silly; it is like a rocking chair: "It keeps you busy, but it won't go nowhere!"

What do you worry about? Here are some of the things I've discovered:

40% of folks worry about things that never happen.

50% of folks worry about things that can never be changed.

10% of folks worry about petty things that don't matter anyway.

8% of folks worry about things that really matter.

So, today we are gonna hear what Jesus has to say about worry. We are gonna see worry through the eyes of Jesus. I hope it will help us not to worry so much—which is something else for me to worry about! I guess I might get kicked out of the Don't Worry Club!

OBSERVATIONS ON THE TEXT

Our hope for life lies in the amazing grace of God. In a sense we have all fallen under a curse of worry. The love of Jesus breaks that curse.

An ambassador was having trouble falling asleep, worrying about all that was happening in his country. His butler asked him, "Sir, can you trust God to govern the world when you are out of it?" The ambassador responded with a rousing "Undoubtedly!"—and then turned over and fell into a deep sleep. "Have a good slumber," the butler responded as he turned out the light and closed the door.

When we seek first the Kingdom of God, there is nothing to worry about.

Jesus saw the city and was troubled in his soul. He saw the greed, the cruelty, the violations of human personalities. Jesus saw the conflicts in corporations, in politicians, in the races. He was moved to tears. The plight of man is worth worrying about. If we make the Kingdom of God our priority, there is nothing to worry about. The hymn says it best: "Oh, what peace we often forfeit, oh what needless pain we bear. All because we do not carry, everything to God in prayer."

When we truly live in Jesus, we live a life of faith and deep commitment. We become dependent totally on God for all parts of our lives. We become independent from things. We know that things won't endure or satisfy. Let us not be distracted, but instead follow Jesus. Jesus has promised to be with us always.

Who is at the center of your worry pattern? If you are trying to carry all of your worries, where do you put God?

Worry for a Christian is useless, needless, and insulting to God. These things that I worry about feel so tremendous that I think they are even too hard for Jesus to handle. I know better, but I still worry. I must be brought to the place of dependence on God. I must clear out everything so there is nothing but God in my soul. I must throw off pride. I must throw off self-sufficiency. I must confess my arrogance and fully lean on him.

Observations and Opportunities

The Christian will let worry be a stimulus for positive action. The energy for this worry should not be wasted. The energy of worry should be used as a spark plug toward doing something positive for Jesus.

The Christian will make his worries "other-centered." Rather than being so self-centered and self-sufficient, let us put our energies toward Kingdom matters. Jesus said, "Don't be anxious!" We are called to dedicate our worrying to thinking about others and not ourselves. We are called to pray for the world consistently and honestly.

The Christian will let worry become a signal for prayer. The Comforter is beside us. So, when you find yourself worrying, stop and pray. Make sure also to worship, to work, and to wait. God is about making all things work together for good. Our job is to pray, to do what we can, and then wait to see how God makes it all good.

OPPORTUNITIES FOR DAILY LIVING

- What worries keep you awake or wake you up in the middle of the night?
- Are they personal inconveniences, embarrassments, failures, injustices, insecurities?

It is good for us to keep God at the center of our lives. Then we can sleep through the night! Set aside your pride. Become more dependent on God. Know the peace of Jesus.

The plight of man is worth worrying about. If Jesus was moved to tears, so should not we?

- Where do you see things worth worrying over—in politics, business, our city, race relations, business relations?
- How can you set aside worry and become more active in finding a solution?
- Who is at the center of your worry pattern? Family? Yourself? Friends?
- If you are carrying the worry, where does that put God?

Too many of us set God aside when we are worrying. We have to be willing to be more dependent on God.

- How can you become more dependent on God?
- How can you take the energy of worry and turn it into doing good for others?
- How can your worry signal that it's time to pray?

Stay open and receptive to God's Spirit.

PRAYER

Thank you, O God, for a good night's sleep. Thank you for allowing me to turn my worries over to you and for your being so gracious to accept them. Bless all the dear children in your tender care. Amen.

The golden rule
Matthew 7:1-12

OPENING

When Jesus sat down to teach, this was an official important act. We speak of a professor's chair. The pope speaks *ex cathedra* from his seat. We talk about the seat of power. Often Jesus spoke when he was walking or standing, but when he sat down this signified that what he was about to say was important.

Matthew 5–7 is what we know as the Sermon on the Mount. Matthew 5:1 says, "When Jesus saw the crowds, he went up on the mountain and he *sat down* and began to teach them. . ." Today, Jesus is teaching us one of his most meaningful lessons: the golden rule.

OBSERVATIONS ON THE TEXT

Relationship with others: Jesus speaks of the error of being judgmental. The rabbis had six great laws that bought them great credit with God: study, visit the sick, be hospitable, be devoted in prayer, educate children in the law, and think the best of others. Kindness in judging others was considered a sacred duty.

Relationship with God: We are to keep asking and seeking. God continues to affirm being with us as we seek answers. Jesus continually assures us of the everlasting, overwhelming love of God. "If you then who are evil give good gifts, how much better will your heavenly parent give good gifts?" We cannot out-give God. Even in our most generous moments, God gives so much more. All of us are recipients of God's goodness.

The golden rule is a centerpiece of this part of the Sermon on the Mount. It is only one verse, but very powerful. Here, Jesus is talking directly about how we relate to one another. This is how we are to relate to Christians and non-Christians, rich and poor, people of different colors and economic status. This "rule" is not exclusive to Jesus.

The great philosophers of the world all state this in some way. Most of them state it in the negative: "What is hateful to yourself, do to no other." The psalmist, Confucius, Socrates, Tobit, Hillel—all teach this principle. They all state it in the negative: "Do not!"

Anyone can satisfy this teaching by doing nothing. They would be "good," but they would be useless. Goodness that consists of doing nothing would be a contradiction of everything Jesus taught. Jesus always calls us to action. Jesus calls us to DO SOMETHING!

Relationships matter. You cannot be in a relationship with someone and be detached. We need each other. This is what the church is really about. There are those who see faith as having correct belief and correct doctrine but who cannot relate to their brothers and sisters in the church. "By this shall all men know that you are my disciples . . . that you love one another" (John 13:35).

The golden rule is the one principle of life that spurs us on to action. If we did nothing else, we could change the world if we live by the Golden Rule. This principle can be applied in settling race problems, domestic troubles, relations between management and labor, relations between political rivals, controlling business competition. Instead of refraining from doing bad things to others, think of something good you would like for someone else to do for you. Then, go and do that for someone else.

OPPORTUNITIES FOR DAILY LIVING

Someone right now needs you to apply this principle in your relationship with them. Think about something you need, then go and do this for someone else. Do it not necessarily for someone in your own group. We all experience conflict in some way or another. Go to someone and do something for or with them and strengthen your relationships.

- Who is waiting for you to "Golden Rule" them?

We get out of life what we pour into it. If we frown at life, it frowns at us. If we heap poisonous criticisms into it, it brings poison back upon us. Revenge often breeds revenge, and condemnation brings condemnation. If we greet life with goodwill, a harvest of goodwill comes back. Sometimes we have pain and delay, but goodwill brings goodwill. And through it all, God is with us.

- What are you pouring into your life?
- How can you shift your thinking?
- What world problem would you like to help solve?

In biblical times when a teacher sat down, it signified that something official and important was about to take place. Teachers spoke from their hearts when sitting; teachers spoke sacred truths when sitting. Jesus was sitting when he delivered the Sermon on the Mount. This teaching brings us important insights on how to relate to one another and to God. In fact, at the end of the Sermon on the Mount, Matthew says the people were "amazed!"

- What about God amazes you?
- How can your relationships become amazing?

PRAYER

Forgive us, O God, when we think ourselves more important than you. Forgive us when we stand to illustrate our power. Forgive us when we judge others. Forgive us when we are better at doing nothing rather than trying to do something. Help us, God, to pour into life the love you have freely given to us through Jesus the Christ. Amen.

The demands of relationships
Matthew 10:21-35

OPENING

Within 30 years of the Cross event, the message of the risen Christ had swept across the known world. Matthew was writing between 80 and 90 AD, while the church was hoping for the imminent return of Jesus, the Second Coming. The church latched onto every opportunity that could be a sign of this second coming.

Today we are still waiting. There are some among us who are also latching on to every opportunity to interpret the Second Coming. The truth is that none of us knows when Jesus will return. What we do know is that we are to be living in peace and loving one another. Until Christ lives in the hearts of men and women, the return will not happen.

OBSERVATIONS ON THE TEXT

Relationship is critical. Jesus tells his disciples that if they want to be in the "inner circle," they must we willing to share in the glory *and* the sufferings of Jesus. There will be glory (which the disciples hoped for in some form or fashion) and sufferings (which the disciples denied). The same is true for us today. We are also his disciples.

What are we hoping for? What do we think will happen to us as we follow Jesus? There may not be "glory" in what we do, but there will be times of challenge.

Be bold in your faith. Jesus calls his disciples to endure (v. 22). This is more than mere survival. This is an active, strong act of living through the hard times. We don't "endure" as Christians; we fight with all our will to stay faithful and present a positive witness. We endure faithfully to the very end of our strength. Some days that will be enough, and some days we will need others around us to survive.

Think about who gives you the will to endure and who you are helping to survive.

Acknowledge your relationship with Jesus. This is not a one-time verbal acknowledgement. This is an ongoing life experience. We can live in denial by indulging in pettiness, dishonesty, lack of charity, bitterness, and even hatred. We live in denial simply by failing to care what happens to those not in our "circle." We are called to be salt and light in our societal circles and in the world. If we are not acknowledging Jesus every day, we might as well be saying, "Yes, I'm a follower of Christ but not so you can tell. I don't let my faith interfere with anything I want to do."

You cannot be a "secret" follower of Jesus. This is a relationship. When we acknowledge Jesus in our everyday lives we are saying, "Yes, sir, Jesus is my Lord!" And then, at the appointed time, Jesus will say to God, "Yes, this is my brother or sister." I don't know about you, but I look forward to that day.

This will be a costly relationship. As we acknowledge our relationship with Jesus, we may lose the natural affection of our families. Self-denial means that we may have to sacrifice personal ambition, family luxury, comfort, or a special career. Following Jesus means there is always some cross we will have to carry. All of us can look backward in our lives and see instances when we have either sacrificed for the Kingdom of God or have denied its existence. Jesus knows that following him will not necessarily bring peace at first. But ultimately, the world will be made right.

In my ministry with you, I see this over and over. Many of you deny yourselves and pick up the burdens of others in our group. What an example some of you are! You carry your own cross and the crosses of others with a daily attitude of living unselfishly. You do this with joy. You don't make martyrs of yourselves; you truly share unconditionally.

OPPORTUNITIES FOR DAILY LIVING

We can hoard our lives if we wish. But if we do so, we will lose all that makes life valuable both to God and to others around us. It is a waste of time and energy, even a waste of faith, to try to hang on to all that God has given us. What makes life valuable is giving generously to those around us. Having a relationship with God may be costly, but it is worth the cost. And, the neat part of it all is that we are free to choose. Like Joshua, we can say "as for my family, we choose God."

- Who needs to have you say to them today, "I value you"?
- Who needs to know that you choose God?
- Who needs you to "choose" a relationship with them even though it may be costly?

Relationships are critical in our faith.

- On a scale of 1-10, where 1 is "not at all" and 10 is "all in/sold out," how do you grade your relationship with Jesus?
- What needs to change in order for you to grow more deeply as Jesus' disciple?
- Are you willing to share in both glory and suffering?
- How do you grade your relationship with your spouse? Your children? Your neighbors?

No one is forgotten by God. Everyone counts for something. There is no mass production in God's world. All of us are specialty handicrafts. So it is that God cares for all of his creation—even a sparrow that costs only half a cent. God cares not only for the bird, but also knows each time that bird flies or hops on the ground. God cares for all of the sparrow's activity. And so it is with us. God values us so much more than we value ourselves.

- What will it take for you to value yourself?

PRAYER

Help us, O God, to see the value in everyone and everything around us. Forgive us for our arrogance in trying to hoard our lives. Forgive us for wanting the rewards and glory without the costs of suffering. Help us, Lord, to live more fully in our relationship with you and with one another and even in our relationships with all of creation. And help us to say to others that they are valued. Most of all, help us to *hear* that we are valued by others and by you. Amen.

Forgiveness without limits
Matthew 18:21-35

OPENING

Life is like a motion picture that can be shown only once. There is no rewind operation in our lives. We cannot live a single moment again. Words spoken are spoken for eternity. We cannot undo anything we've done or do anything we've missed doing. So, it behooves us to carefully guard our relationships every day.

Something had damaged the apostle Peter's relationship with a friend. He asked Jesus a question that sounds a lot like us. Perhaps he was tired of trying to mend this relationship, or perhaps he was just disgusted with the whole relationship. He asked, "Just how many times do I have to forgive this friend?" (The rabbis of the day insisted that three attempts at forgiveness and restoration were enough.) Peter probably didn't get the response he was expecting!

What do we do with our regrets? What do we do about those relationships we have damaged? How do we forgive and forget and move forward? How many times are we willing to try to forgive and restore hurt or broken relationships?

OBSERVATIONS ON THE TEXT

70 x 7: Peter responded to Jesus with the number 7 as the limit for forgiveness, thinking that Jesus would consider him noble. Peter thought that going more than double the rabbinical expectation, he would be complimented by Jesus. Instead, Jesus responded with 70 times 7! Who counts that high in trying to forgive and restore friendship?

Jesus, the master storyteller, illustrated his words with a story. Jesus tells us there is no way to atone for all the wrongs we have committed toward God or others. However, we can change our heart and move forward with changed behaviors. Jesus says there is no limit on the number of times we should try to rebuild broken relationships. No matter how hard this may be, we keep trying.

Changed behaviors come from changed hearts. Changes come because of our love for God. We love because God first loved us. And so, we do whatever it takes for as long as it takes to reconcile and restore. A burdened heart with grudges cannot offer God wholeness or adoration. There are three parts to real forgiveness:

The injured party has to accept the hurt. We do ourselves no good when we deny or ignore our pain. Most of the hurts we bear from others are not that important. But we still cannot deny the pain or gloss over the pain. To do so causes us further hurt—and lets the offender off the hook!

The injured party may have to help the offender realize the painful action. Whether the hurt was intended and vicious or unintended, we who have been hurt should go to them. We say something to them like, "I have been hurt by your actions. And, I am going to bear it responsibly." Perhaps we can grow into the mind like the mind Joseph had toward his brothers: "You sold me into slavery. That hurt me. But don't be angry with yourselves for this" (Gen. 45:5).

The injured party restores understanding, rebuilding fellowship and showing goodwill to the offender. Jesus puts reconciliation above everything. Reconciliation is a continuing imperative. Confronting the offender is not to shame or condemn, but to restore fellowship. Forgiveness is to be redemptive in nature, so we forgive in love. In the same way that Jesus took the towel and washed the disciples' feet, let us take up a towel and do the same to those who have hurt us.

God's forgiveness is linked to our own. There is no escaping the truth of this parable. God's forgiveness and our own forgiveness are linked together. Jesus has told us that only the merciful will be forgiven. If a person says, "I'll never forgive you for this," then the relationship between the injured party and God is also injured. An unforgiving spirit shuts the door between us and God. For the one who says, "I never forgive," we can only respond, "Then I hope you never sin." (Reportedly, this is what John Wesley said to General Oglethorpe.)

I'm not sure about you, but I need and desire God's forgiveness. I'm not willing to risk losing God's love because of some trivial grudge. Forgiving is a matter of the heart; forgetting is a matter of the mind. Most that passes for forgiveness is often not that at all. Forgiveness is an event—not just an idea. When God forgives, something drastic happens. We know that God removes confessed sin as far as the east is from the west. How far is that? And, God also forgets. God promises to blot out our sin.

Many of us forgive and believe that we have truly forgiven. Our forgiveness is from the heart. But we have more trouble in forgetting. True forgiveness also forgets. Forgiveness will break the circle of hate and can truly change us. When we truly forgive, we also truly forget. Forgiving is costly, but forgiving (and forgetting) is worth the cost.

OPPORTUNITIES FOR DAILY LIVING

A certain woman discovered that her husband was having an affair with a woman in his office. The husband finally came to his senses, asked forgiveness from his wife, and declared his love for her and their children. The wife told her pastor, "I just can't forgive this. I don't think I can get past it." The pastor replied, "Jesus bore our sins in his body on the cross. The sinner will always suffer. Help your husband bear his burden of sin."

The wife knew that forgiveness must happen for them to move on in their marriage. She went to her husband and responded, "I have been hurt deeply by your actions. And I realize that you know you have hurt us." She then asked him, with sincerity, for forgiveness for abandoning him in his loneliness and pain.

A genuine forgiving spirit is one of the most God-like characteristics a person can reflect!

- Who needs your forgiveness today?
- Who needs your forgetfulness today?

PRAYER

God, you never promised that life would be easy. You never promised that our lives would be without hurt and pain. But God, life is too short and your love is eternal. Help us to live in your love, forgiving the sin and forgetting the pain. Help us, please, O God! Amen.

The things to come
Matthew 24

OPENING

From the beginning of time, curiosity has played a great part in the history of the world. Curiosity is both good and bad. Properly exercised, curiosity can whet an appetite for knowledge. Negatively, it can cause us to meddle in another's affairs. But curiosity about the future is something that pulls at all of us. Today, we hear Jesus talking about things to come. Here is an outline:

-The destruction of Jerusalem (vv. 1-2, 15-20):

    Jesus was right! As he predicted, the temple was destroyed and Jerusalem fell in 70 AD.

-Persecutions to come (vv. 9-14):

    Jesus was right. His followers would endure heartbreaking and soul-searing sufferings.

-Dangers of last days (vv. 3-6, 21-22):

    Jesus was right. The Christian faith would be twisted and falsified by false prophets.

-Warning of the Second Coming (vv. 7-8, 24-27):

    Jesus wanted to impress us with the importance of this. He used the same language as did the prophets of the Old Testament and the apocalyptic writers.

-A call to be watchful (vv. 28-37):

    As men live in the shadow of eternity with the constant possibility of God's intervention, there is a necessity to be ever ready.

OBSERVATIONS ON THE TEXT

There is not one time in biblical or secular history when prophecy has been completely understood *before* it came to pass. This drama in which we live is going to come to a fitting climax. He who began a good work will finish it. The author will step on the stage when the final curtain has been rung down and make sense of things formerly misunderstood. Jesus is speaking about last things, not to write history ahead of time, but to reassure, strengthen, and equip his followers. Jesus wants us to know that God is aware of what's happening and that God is at work.

These country Galileans staggered at the beauty of the temple. It was one of the wonders of the world. Herod began building it in 20 BC, and it was still being finished in Jesus' time. Josephus gives some details:

    Some stones were 40 ft. x 12 ft. x 18 ft.

    The entrance was by way of a bridge 50 ft. wide x 354 ft. long.

    The royal porch had a double row of Corinthian columns 37.5 ft. high.

    The outward face of the temple was gold-plated. (Thus, the reflection of the rising sun was too bright to look upon.)

Could it be that Jesus was more interested in the quality of life than the quantity or elegance of things? So much for man's permanence! The temple was ultimately destroyed. Jesus warned his hearers, "When you see the devastation begin, flee to the mountains" (v. 16). But they did just the opposite. History tells us that 97,000 people were taken captive and that more than 1,000,000 died of starvation. The streets were filled with swollen dead bodies. Those alive were too weak to work. The Romans came to make a statement—and they did!

Observations and Opportunities

Jesus' followers would experience deep sufferings. There is a sense in which the church will always be persecuted in an unchristian society. How much can we take without denying our faith?

Some people betrayed members of their families who were believers. Some informed on their friends. Survival would be the way of life, holding out for their faith in God.

False leaders would suddenly appear on the scene seeking followers. Many a religious movement feeds off the ego of its leader. The egotists try to steal the Christian name, but the purity of faith always wins. A prime example is Jim Jones and the mess created at Jonestown in South Africa. There are always two characteristics to watch out for in these false prophets: one who tries to promote his own version of the truth and one who tries to attach men to himself rather than to God.

What in our current world are threats to our faith? How are we defending the church and our faith?

OPPORTUNITIES FOR DAILY LIVING

Take heart, O Christian! God has not abandoned the world. God will intervene at points. Do not be discouraged over the escalation of evil. This is a prelude to re-creation. Judgment and redemption are certain. Jesus is coming again, and his return will be swift and sudden. The time when Jesus will return is locked in God's heart. It is blasphemy to think we know more than God. His return will be public, not secret.

What are we to do with what Jesus says? We are to help everyone get ready. We are to live so that when we see Jesus face-to-face, we will not be embarrassed or hysterical. I know I will be *very* excited and *very* happy to see my Savior.

Stay alert and live without procrastination so that others will recognize your faith and want to know how to receive the same. We believe in a God who has said he *would*, a God whom we know *can*, and a God who *will* keep his promises.

PRAYER

God of yesterday, today, and the days to come, we thank you this day for the knowledge that, in the midst of pain and agony, you are indeed the perfect parent to your children. You will love us unconditionally and with grace. You will prepare a place for us even in the presence of our enemies. Your son, Jesus, is coming again. Thanks be to God. Amen.

In remembrance
Matthew 26:1-56

OPENING

As sports teams do prior to a major game, they have a confidence-building session in the locker room before going on the field. The University of Alabama has over its exit door to the field a very large "WIN" sign. As each man leaves for the field, he extends his arm high to give the sign a whack expressing his personal confidence.

We enjoy being in the company of confident people. On a scale of 1 to 10, with 10 being very high, how would you rate your confidence factor?

Society is built upon trust, and trust upon confidence, especially the confidence we have in our leaders. We hold leaders to a higher standard. We expect them to have high integrity. We expect them to be confident. We expect to be able to trust them! Integrity, confidence, and trust cannot be compelled into another. We cannot order someone to have these traits. Jesus had all these traits and more. Let's examine them in the midst of the chaos of Holy Week.

OBSERVATIONS ON THE TEXT

Jesus certainly had high integrity, deep confidence, and trusted leadership. He had an inner peace he wanted us to have. In John 14:27, Jesus gives us this wish: "Peace I leave with you, not as the world gives; let not your heart be troubled." The peace of Jesus came from his heavenly father. And if God gives this peace to Jesus, certainly the gift is available to us, *if* we are willing to accept the gift and develop our traits of integrity, confidence, and trust that lead to this peace. This peace served Jesus well in the days before his trial, crucifixion, death, and resurrection. This peace will also serve us well as we go through our own trials and struggles.

The disciples needed this depth of peace. Their hopes for an earthly king who would overthrow the hated Romans were dashed to bits. They are in Jerusalem. The time is just before Passover, commemorating God's deliverance from the 10th plague upon Egypt for the freeing of Israel from slavery. Some scholars estimate that the Passover crowd in Jerusalem during this week was almost 3 million people. That was some party! So, the chief priests and scribes wanted to wait until after Passover to grab hold of Jesus—after the party was over and the tourists had gone home. You see, Jesus had become quite the celebrity at this point.

In verse 6 an unnamed woman anoints Jesus with expensive oil—worth a year's salary. Presumably she was thinking she was anointing him for kingship, but Jesus knew his coronation would be a crown of thorns and his throne a cross. This anointing raised two different responses.

The disciples were angry and criticized her for wasting such expensive oil. "Why this waste? This ointment could have been sold for a large sum and the money given to the poor" (v. 8). Jesus complimented her by saying she had done a beautiful thing. He knew the anointing was not in preparation for a coronation but for a cross.

Verses 26-29 are some of the most beloved in our faith. "This is my body" was completely symbolic even as when Jesus said, "I am the door." He was not referring to himself literally but in metaphor. His disciples would have completely understood the setting and the meaning. The cup he shared was not a cup of fear; it too was symbolic. This would be a cup of physical pain, of total rejection. Just as the Mosaic covenant was sealed with the blood of an animal, the new covenant was sealed in Jesus' own blood. There are many theories in other faiths about the representative nature of the Supper. However, I believe that Jesus was clearly teaching that the Supper is the *vehicle* whereby we receive the grace and love of God's forgiveness.

Not only is the Supper the deeply meaningful ritual of forgiveness each time we partake, but it is also a time when we remember the deep sacrifice Jesus and God made for the world. The materials involved in the Lord's Supper link us to an event that occurred long ago. These same materials link us to God and what God has done for us. And, these materials restore the joy of our salvation each time we come to the Lord's table.

OPPORTUNITIES FOR DAILY LIVING

"Truly I tell you, wherever this good news is proclaimed in the whole world, what she has done will be told in remembrance of her" (v. 13). And so the story continues. We don't know this woman, her name, her life. But we know Jesus trusted her, we know she had confidence, and we know she did a beautiful thing.

- Who do you trust?
- Would you have had the confidence to approach Jesus and anoint him?
- Who would you have the confidence to respond to in our class with such love and support?

Notice the unnamed people in this passage. The woman who anointed Jesus is not named. The man who supplied the room for the Passover dinner is not named. In a world where so many of us are clamoring for fame and fortune, these two unnamed people were central to the ministry of Jesus in his last days.

- What is so enticing about fame?
- Why do so many people want to be famous?
- If you could claim fame, for what would you want to be famous? Why?

How can those of us who are unnamed and unnoticed make a difference for our God in the same ways the man and woman of Matthew 26 did? The movements in these verses are not placed here just for a historical record of the last days of Jesus. They are placed here for us to have absolute confidence in the leadership of God. The first Lord's Supper was not a farewell but a pledge of confidence in the new covenant. This promise leads us to confidence, integrity, and trust. This confidence allows us to "whack" the imaginary sign over our door as we take the field each day.

- What word is on your sign?
- How does this word give you confidence to share Jesus, build trust, and live with integrity?

PRAYER

Forgive me, God, when I seek fame and fortune at the expense of others. Forgive me when I put my own arrogance and greed before strengthening my integrity, deepening trust, and inspiring confidence in the world. Help me, please, oh God, to remember you, not just at the Supper but every day. Amen.

Betrayal
Matthew 26:57-67, 27:1-26

OPENING

We pick up today with the trial of Jesus. There seems to have been three parts to this trial: the night at the high priest's house, the same place but first thing in the morning, and at Pilate's house.

Being under the civil rule of Rome, the Jewish court had no authority to carry out a death sentence—only a Roman court could do this. When morning came, a legal meeting was held and the decision made to put Jesus to death. A charge of blasphemy was decided as Jesus claimed to be the Messiah. Jesus carefully avoided using the name of God for himself—the strict definition for blasphemy—but the deck was already stacked against him.

In every way, Jewish court procedure was violated. The third trial took place at Pilate's house. Pilate did have the authority to acquit or condemn, but the charge of blasphemy had little interest for him. Jesus was of no interest to him. However, when the charge was changed from "son of God" to "king of the Jews," Pilate's ego and position were challenged. Pilate had been in trouble with Rome before. He was not on the most solid of ground. A Jewish uprising would not sit well with Rome. So he asked the crowd, "What shall I do with Jesus?" He knew the crowd was riled up; the choice would be an easy one. Too often, people can be stirred up with just a few inflammatory words. Pilate knew the psychology of the crowd. Let's look closely at the events of this week.

OBSERVATIONS ON THE TEXT

We cannot help but ask, "Where were all the people Jesus had healed, had raised from the dead, had fed on the hillside?" Why were all the friends of Jesus silent?

When good people do nothing, evil triumphs easily. Jesus was subjected to physical pain, emotional pain, great violence, and mockery. We have to fight the temptation to do nothing. We have to fight the temptation to be bitter or to respond in unchristian ways when people hurt us. We look at Jesus going through all this evil, and it puts us in good company.

There are three main characters in this drama. I'd like to look at each of them and see that they have some descendants in our modern world.

To unload his sense of guilt, Judas tried to return the money to his co-conspirators. The strange thing about sin is that a man can come to hate the very thing he has gained. No doubt the calmness with which Jesus submitted to arrest, the look of dismay on the faces of the other disciples, the expression on Jesus' face at the Passover feast, and Jesus' reproving questions in the garden must have haunted Judas through the night and early morning. He didn't have the courage to return to the apostles. He tried to give back the money. He loudly confessed he had betrayed innocent blood. His confessions were to his fellow conspirators, not to the one who he had wronged—not to God, not even to himself. Judas was trying to force Jesus into the pursuit of nationalism. He knew Jesus could lead a rebellion against Rome, and the Jews could overthrow Rome. And when Jesus refused, Judas betrayed him. And Judas ultimately took his own life!

Pilate was an arrogant and insulting administrator. He loved his position and would do anything to protect it. He knew Jesus was not a threat to Rome, but he also knew Jesus was a threat to his own power. He also knew it was a betrayal of Roman law to sentence an innocent man to death. But, after trying to get the crowd to reconsider, he gave in to the pressure of the Jews.

Observations and Opportunities

Luke says Pilate twice declared he could find no fault in Jesus. John says three times he made protest. He could have saved Jesus' life, but the death of Jesus was the safer move for his own career. So, he washed his hands of the whole affair. He compromised his integrity for self-interest.

While Jesus was being tried before Caiaphas, Simon Peter underwent a trial of his own. If ever there was an incident one would like to cover up, this is it. His love had led him to follow Jesus. His fear had led him to deny him. Peter must have told this story on himself in the days and years to come. It does do him some honor that he was brave enough to tell this. He walked into the courtyard and denied Jesus three times. He was not leaving—he wanted to be near Jesus—but he cowered in the shadows. His denial was not premeditated, but his fear was palpable. And then he heard the cock crow, and a fire was set to his conscience. Jesus' look was his undoing, and he broke into tears.

OPPORTUNITIES FOR DAILY LIVING

Have you ever compromised your integrity for what seemed best for you at the time? I have, and I've never forgotten this lesson. For five years during the Depression I worked for a doctor. I was paying my own way at the university night school. To protect my job, the doctor falsified information to the IRS to keep down expenses. I went along with this to protect my job. I am still sick about it to this day. To compromise your values even to protect yourself is not right under any circumstances. Personal integrity is the most important character trait we have. I'm not asking for verbal testimonies, but I am asking for your internal thoughtfulness about this.

Legend has it that Peter never heard a rooster crow after that "denial morning" that he did not break into tears. Even though he would be forgiven by the risen Christ, his heart remained broken. His weeping was a continued sign of a broken heart, even though he had repented and had been forgiven.

- How are you like Judas?
- When might you have tried to force a friend into an issue of your own selfishness?
- How are you like Pilate?
- When might you have sacrificed your integrity to protect your own self-interest?
- How are you like Simon Peter?
- What might make your weep, remind you of your brokenness when you have denied Jesus?

We all have a bit of Judas, Pilate, and Simon Peter in us. But the best news is that we all have *more* of Jesus in us than the rest of the other three. We are all doers of the gospel. We are all followers of the risen Jesus. We are all forgiven. Easter reminds us of the greatness of God—grace that is greater than all our sin!

PRAYER

Thank you, God, for the Easter blessing. Thank you for reminding me of my arrogance, my greed, and my cowardice. Thank you, even more, for reminding me in a powerful way of my salvation. He is risen. He is risen indeed!

A new life for Nicodemus
John 3:1-16

OPENING

For the most part as we follow Jesus through the Gospels, we see him surrounded by ordinary people. But today he visits with one of the 400, the aristocracy of Jerusalem.

Nicodemus was a Pharisee, a trained theologian who sincerely tried to please God by observing every law. When he became a Pharisee, he pledged to live every detail of the law. The Pharisees seemed to have grown out of the time of the exile when the Jews deprived of entering the temple had lay lawyers who kept them in touch with their law, the first five books of the Old Testament.

Though the Pharisees claimed that the law was complete in these first five books, all one really needed was to live a good life. Yet it was too general, and so they developed regulations to cover every situation conceivable in the lives of the children of Israel. The Pharisees took things to the extreme to keep people from "sin." Much of this was beyond absurd.

Jesus came to fulfill the law, not do away with the law. He stressed that the law was made for man, not man for the law. God did not expect perfection; God expected faithfulness. This is the conversation we get to eavesdrop on today: Jesus and Nicodemus . . . fascinating!

OBSERVATIONS ON THE TEXT

Nicodemus is not your typical Bible person, especially where Jesus is concerned. He is wealthy. He is a member of the Sanhedrin, the 70 top leaders of Israel who make up the supreme court. He has power, prestige, and influence, not to mention wealth. It is amazing that such an aristocrat from a good family would come to a homeless prophet who used to be a carpenter and talk to him about his soul, his spiritual life, and his eternal life. Apparently he has been so impressed by the work and words of Jesus that he wants to know more. This is one of the most tremendous chapters in the Bible.

Nicodemus asks a question of identity, and in verse 3 Jesus answers: "Very truly I tell you" (NRSV) / "Truly, Truly" (RSV) / "I assure you" (Philips) / "With all the sincerity I possess" (Living Bible). Basically, Jesus says: "Here is the truth that I confirm and affirm with all of my being." Then Jesus moves to the *big* answer: "You must be born from above, anew, again. . ." Jesus says to Nicodemus that seeing the Kingdom is more than observing the law; Jesus is promising a depth of experience. Life must be oriented toward God, experienced. "All you know and think about must be centered in God. What you have, what you have experienced, what you have attained, mean nothing. Only God means everything."

Yet Nicodemus does not understand: "How can a man be born again?" And Jesus gives another "truly truly" answer: "Again, Nick, here's what I'm saying with all my heart and soul and being. Here's the truth Nicodemus, 'You must be born of water and Spirit!'" Basically, Jesus is saying to Nicodemus: "This is a cleansing purification. This is a purifying so deep that your insides are made new. So repent, turn your life around, be transformed by the love of God!"

In verse 8 Jesus tells Nicodemus that in a new physical birth everything is brand new. In spiritual birth the same is true. And, the most important part of being made new, as a physical or spiritual being, is obedience: We say to God we love you, and then we show God our love through our obedience. (Can you imagine saying to someone, "I love you," and then purposely doing things that grieve and hurt the loved one? This newness is a totally new lifestyle.)

And then comes the kicker: "God so loved the world that he gave his only son, so that everyone who believes in him may not perish but may have eternal life" (John 3:16). Jesus initiates this part of the conversation. God loves the world fully, totally. His concern is of such height and depth and length and breadth that it would involve suffering of the one whom he loves intensely.

What would it take for you to deliberately expose your child to participate painfully in a solution to free other children? Why did God do it? Because God loves and God acts. We are incomplete in our capacities to love, but in God we have begun a journey toward growth. One theologian put it like this: "Jesus took life in both of his hands, and what he made of it made people want an eternity of it."

OPPORTUNITIES FOR DAILY LIVING

A life fit for eternity is above anything we might know about. Jesus shows us the Father, the character of the one who is responsible, and on God's face is a smile. It is obvious from the teaching of Jesus that he was fully aware of the world. His stories came from the birds of the air, the lilies of the field, the times of planting and seeding, the wonder of sunshine and rain and wind and light and salt. Nothing went unnoticed by Jesus. But mostly, Jesus was fully aware of people. He embraced Nicodemus when he could have rejected him. He spent time with Nicodemus, loved him, and brought him to the throne of God.

- Who needs you in the way that Nicodemus needed Jesus?

Ultimately, the Pharisees would put Jesus through humiliation, physical pain, and death. Jesus knew all this would happen but did not let anything get in the way of his love and worship of God. Jesus did not let anyone get in the way of God's Kingdom. Jesus never missed an opportunity to share how to be born again, how to have eternal life.

It seems to me that we may have gotten away from these kinds of relationships. I don't know about you, but I want eternal life and all eternity. And when we receive this gift, God smiles! I can't wait to see that smile someday. What about you?

PRAYER

Thank you, God, for Jesus. Thank you, God, for loving us enough to give your most precious Son for our benefit. Thank you, God, for Jesus. And thank you, God, for the gift of eternal life through Jesus, our Christ. Amen.

Sight vs. seeing
John 9:1-12

OPENING

If you had been blind since birth and then given sight, how would you feel? If you had been blind since birth, how would you describe an egg? How would you know about the yellow and white? How would you describe the difference between scrambled and poached, an Easter egg and a robin's egg?

Imagine the startling effect of one who had never seen his mother's face, a friend, a river, a tree, a sunset. Imagine seeing the world around you for the first time ever! Read John 9:1-7 and just think on the implications of this miracle for a minute.

And now hear the question from the apostles: "How could this blindness be? Was this due to his own sin before he was born? Was this due to his own sin the moment he was born? Was this due to the sin of his mother or his father?" And then the conversations began!

OBSERVATIONS ON THE TEXT

If sin didn't cause this man's blindness, then what was the reason? Jesus would say that he was in the right place at the right time with the right person so that this healing could show God's grace, compassion, and power.

It is only when life deals us a terrible blow, when trouble and disaster fall, that Jesus can show the world how a Christian can live. In the midst of trouble and stress, a Christian can live with beauty, endurance, and nobility. Our task is to live with grace in the world, giving witness to the same grace, compassion, and power that Jesus did. Any kind of suffering or opposition is an opportunity for us to show the world the power of God within us.

Some questions have popped into my mind: Why did Jesus spit in the ground and make mud? Why did the neighbors take the man to the Pharisees? What was their motive? Why weren't the Pharisees excited when the man received sight?

When Jesus spread the "holy mud" on the man's eyes and told him, "Go wash," I can imagine the blind man having all kinds of whiny responses: "Why should I? Just wash me here! It's too far. Just wash me here! I've just come from there. You want me to fight traffic to go back? Just wash me here! Who do you think you are? It's not going to work anyway. Just WASH ME HERE!"

That's just like us. We have so many excuses for not obeying. The healing virtue of Jesus is that he was always doing the unexpected. The serendipity of Jesus always got people's attention. In Jesus' day, saliva was thought to hold many healing properties. And Jesus used this method in other places for healing too.

The neighbors must have known that Jesus was a controversial figure. Certainly there were those who had questions about his credibility. Remember the question, "Can anything good come out of Nazareth?" (John 1:43-46). The neighbors wanted the Pharisees to see this miracle and to pronounce it credible or fraud. And that is also just like us! The neighbors were arguing whether he was even the same man when he came back. So, they brought the man to their spiritual leaders. Then the fun began.

It is one thing when lay persons argue about the work of God; it is something else when our spiritual leaders do so. The Pharisees argued among themselves, and even argued with the blind man. I can hear them saying, "You may be healed, but you were born entirely in sin. And, are you trying to teach us?" So, they drove him out (John 9:34).

Today some of our spiritual leaders are having theological arguments. I can tell you, the Pharisees in our world are not going to see God's miracle either. And, probably, some people will be driven out!

No one who witnessed the healing of the blind man could agree on what happened. The Pharisees saw the results and had arguments (vv. 16-17). This is typical today of those who think *their way* is the way to serve God and to interpret Scripture. The Pharisees *knew* they were the spiritual experts of the day. But their arrogance made them "blind." They were threatened by differences of opinion. They could not see that a changed life was more important than healing, especially healing on the Sabbath. Jesus had ignored religious law to give this man sight. Wow! The Pharisees were really the blind in this story.

The more I see of this man, the better I like him. He was a plain fella, independent, refusing to bow to the threats of the blind religious leaders. He was a man with courage who would not be intimidated. And that takes me back to the opening question: If you had been blind since birth and then given sight, how would you feel? Bold, courageous, blessed—that's how!

OPPORTUNITIES FOR DAILY LIVING

We make excuses even when Jesus is standing right in front of us! We see the miracles but refuse to accept them. We see the Pharisees arguing and wonder why they preferred the law to the blind man right in front of them. Theological arguments are nothing new. These have been happening since the beginning of time. We have to pay close attention to see the truth. We can't be deceived by those who would mislead us because of their arrogance and narrow-mindedness. People matter!

- Where is your blindness?
- What needs to happen to help you see?
- To whom do you listen for the truth?
- How can you keep your eyes on the truth of Jesus and not get distracted by arguments and arrogance?

PRAYER

Lord, give us eyes to see and ears to hear. Forgive us when we see your majesty right in front of us and we refuse to see. Forgive us when we refuse to see Jesus. Lord, help our blindness. Amen.

Blindness
John 9:13-41

OPENING

I continue to be intrigued by this issue of blindness. Notice that the Pharisees said, "We know!" Their arrogance kept them from seeing; they just claimed the authority of their position to discount the healing power of Jesus. Their skepticism carried a veiled threat as well: "If you continue to press this point of being healed, you are going to be in trouble too!" And, believe me, nobody wanted to be personally in trouble with the religious leaders of their day.

The Pharisees were trying to protect the law that they wrote and interpreted. There is no way they could condone healing on the Sabbath. Their knowledge came from their insights into the Scriptures. They paid no attention to the healing of the person. Their job was to make sure the people followed the law. They certainly had no room for a "freelance" prophet running around, healing, doing miracles, challenging their authority—their financial authority, their theological authority, their intellectual authority.

Now notice the man's response: "I don't know!" He said this several times. He had no explanation of what had happened. He was blind one moment. A man spit in the dirt, made mud, placed it on his eyes, and he went for a dip in the pool. As he came up out of the water, he could see! Glory! The man could tell what had happened, but he had no explanation of how. And here is the real issue: A changed life, even a seeking life, can't be argued theologically. Here is the one thing I know: The final and conclusive argument that cannot be refuted is our own experience.

OBSERVATIONS ON THE TEXT

The courage of the blind man angered the Pharisees. They boasted that they followed Moses. They were pretty sure that Jesus was another fraud seeking to take away their authority and power. The blind man basically said, "You are supposed to be the religious experts. Is God finished at work in the world? Would God choose to work through a man who did not belong to God?"

The Pharisees refused to even engage in conversation. "We believe in the first 11 chapters of Genesis. That is enough for us to build a whole religious system upon. It was good enough for Moses; it is good enough for us. We don't know this 'new guy' from Nazareth. He says weird things. He contradicts the law. We don't believe that you have been healed. We're not sure you were ever blind!"

Since the Pharisees could not refute this man, they drove him out of the synagogue and called him a sinner. Jesus heard what had happened and sought the man out. Isn't that just like Jesus? When our churches refuse to let certain people come into our sanctuaries, Jesus says, "Come unto me!" This is characteristic of Jesus. Jesus sought out this one "lost sheep"—a person who had been "thrown out of church"—to bring him to God. If we are lonely, if we are ignored, if we are tossed out, we can be quite certain that Jesus will come seeking us out too.

In verse 41 Jesus makes an interesting point. The physically blind are aware of their condition, but often the spiritually blind are not. The preconceived dogma of the Pharisees kept them from opening their eyes. They chose to stay blind in their dogma. They were not open to the continuing revelation of God.

Observations and Opportunities

Jesus never condemned honest doubt. He always challenged closed minds because closed minds reflected closed hearts. And that was true in this case. The Pharisees were worried about healing on the Sabbath rather than celebrating a blind man receiving sight.

A closed mind and a closed heart reveal the character of a man. We must be careful how we choose what we believe about God. God has always been and will always be surprising us. We have the choice to believe the continuing work of God or to reject it. I don't know about you, but I am keeping my eyes and heart and mind open to God!

OPPORTUNITIES FOR DAILY LIVING
- What testimony does your life give?
- Has God worked miracles in your life?
- How are you representing what God has done in your life?

Jesus sought out the blind man to share the love of God with him.

- Whom are you seeking to share God's love with?

Notice verse 35. Jesus says, "The one you have seen and have heard is the Son of Man." John uses the whole of this man's senses to show us how tuned in to him Jesus was. Jesus knew the man's heart. That was the key!

- What does Jesus see when he looks into your heart?

People pay attention to a phony witness. The purpose of the church is to convey God's message of love to the world. Institutions do not bring people to Christ; people bring people to Christ. Individuals, you, me, his disciples in the world: We are now the ones who have been called to bring sight to the blind. Jesus says that we are the light of the world. Blind people live in darkness.

- What light are you taking to the world?
- How are you sharing your light?

Believe me, the world does take notice!

- How are you like the blind man? His neighbors? His parents? The Pharisees?
- What do you do with verse 41: "If you were blind, you would have no sin. But now that you say you see, your sin remains"?

Some of the Pharisees "hoped" they were good people, and yet, Jesus refused to honor their blindness. We hope that we are good people too, but hoping won't make it so. We've got work to do!

PRAYER

Help us, oh God, to see as you see, to hear as you hear, and to act lovingly as you love. Even though we think we see, help us to know, God, that we don't see everything. Teach us to be more like Jesus. Amen.

Freedom from fear and grief*
John 11, 17:3

OPENING

A pall hovers over our class today. Our minds are preoccupied by a tragedy that has shockingly stalked through our friendships this week. Somehow these scriptures were not speaking to my heart's need. I'm just so pained as I know we all are. Studying God's Word as a child with faith in our hearts, searching for help and comfort, is quite different than studying it in a historical and scholarly manner.

I think we can relate to the apostles today in the midst of this pain. My heart cried out, "Why Lord? *Why?*" I realized the futility of such a question. Too often we ask the wrong questions, knowing there are no answers. Death is the price we pay for being human.

I suppose the real question is, "Lord, what would you have us learn from this overwhelming pain we are experiencing?" So, I invite you to pick and choose whatever seems appropriate. Whatever truth comes from me today is of the Spirit, as it is each week. But today, you need to know this is truly, undeniably from the Spirit. I hope the Spirit will comfort us all today as we comfort one another when we consider the death of Jesus in the mix of our terrible tragedy.

OBSERVATIONS ON THE TEXT

We are reminded that we are given life so that we might have eternal life. This physical life is all too brief. The physical life depends on the community we build with others. This "horizontal" relationship is about loving neighbors, family, friends, and associates. This community is given to us as a support for living our physical lives to the fullest even for the briefest of time.

We were made to support each other. We cannot live in isolation. In crises the friendships we've made carry us. Today in our grief we carry each other and we carry this dear friend who has lost her husband. Let's call her. Let's assure her that she is not alone in her need. We have a source of comfort and of peace.

And, we are reminded again that the "vertical" relationship is the real relationship that matters. This vertical relationship with God is what really sustains us when we face grief like this. And, God has given us the greatest gift beyond Jesus: prayer. Let us pray for one another. Let us pray for our church community and class. Sometimes when people are so grief-stricken, they cannot pray for themselves. Prayer is power, and we are called to pray and to pray powerfully.

Jesus dealt with sorrow too. One of the most profound verses in the Bible is John 11:3. God's compassion is so much more than our compassion. Jesus was moved for many reasons over the death of this friend. I don't know all the feelings Jesus experienced, but I'm sure of all the feelings you and I are experiencing. And, I am confident that God is comforting us, comforting our friend, and crying with us.

Emotions are God-given. Our lives are greatly affected by our emotions, both positively and negatively. Fear, awe, hope, depression, joy, anger, grief, anxiety, love: God can handle our emotions today and every day. We must give our emotions to God.

In verse 21 Martha did so: "Lord, if you had been here, my brother would not have died." God invites us to pour our own heart out to him even if we are struggling with grief, complaints, and bitterness. God can do a lot with us when we are honest. I don't feel like praying, "Thy will be done!" today. I'm hurting, I'm angry, I'm upset, and I don't have any answers.

God takes care of us. God surprises us with answers. Jesus essentially says, "Oh, Martha, I wish I had been here." The important fact is not whether one lives or dies; all that really matters is that Jesus is truly the resurrection and the life—eternal life!

OPPORTUNITIES FOR DAILY LIVING

Eugene O'Neill wrote a little-known play titled *Lazarus Laughed*. It picks up where the biblical story leaves off. The play opens with Lazarus coming out of the grave *laughing*! His laughter is not a scornful kind of laughter, not a jeering kind of laughter. This laughter is a gleeful, soft, and tender kind of sound. He looks around at his family, neighbors, and Jesus. Then he looks to the sky and says softly, "Yes!" He takes delight in all the earthly things around him and in all the people around him. He is at peace.

Perhaps in the days to come we can be as Lazarus. Perhaps we can look to the heavens and feel the love of God. Perhaps we can look around the room at one another today and feel the love of God. God weeps with us today. God will laugh with us in the days to come.

The first words Matthew records of Jesus following the resurrection are, "Be not afraid" (28:10). The resurrection of Jesus was meant to take away our fear—all fear! Too many of us fear life as much as we fear death.

Do you recall how fearlessly Jesus stood before Pilate? Do you recall how fearlessly Jesus confronted Satan in the wilderness? Do you recall how fearlessly Jesus cleared the temple?

In the same ways, Jesus confronted the death of Lazarus and the cross. God has confronted everything we will ever confront. Here is the good news: we have been given freedom from fear. I know we don't feel free today. I am confident, however, that we will feel free in the days ahead. Today we weep, but hopefully in the days ahead we, like Lazarus, will be able to laugh again!

PRAYER

God, we have no words to pray today. We hurt and we trust that you know what we need in our grief and our pain. Please, God, dry our tears, comfort our pain, and help us to laugh again. Amen.

*Evidently, Eula Mae wrote this lesson about the death of Jesus. But during the week before she taught, someone in the class died. So, she wove in the death of Jesus with the death of this dear friend.

Pentecost
Acts 2

OPENING

A friend of mine attending college opened the door to see two tousled-haired, dirt-smeared young boys selling raffle tickets. In bold letters on their T-shirts were the words, "Holy Ghost." My young friend commented, "Wow! As dirty as you are, you must have been wrestling with God's Spirit. What does he look like?" She didn't buy a raffle ticket!

Our understanding and appreciation of God's Holy Spirit is small because our knowledge of the Spirit is small. We want to know what the Spirit looks like. We want to know God by seeing and touching and embracing God. Somehow the Holy Spirit just seems like a cloud floating in the air or the fog that covers the ranch early in the morning. For some, it's just "Holy Smoke!"

Today we are looking at the Holy Spirit who came to us as the Comforter on Pentecost. Was the Spirit with God at creation? Was the Spirit in existence before Pentecost? Well, let's see what the Bible has to say to us. Perhaps we'll get a glance of the Spirit before we're done today.

OBSERVATIONS ON THE TEXT

Pentecost was the day the Christian church was born. This was an amazing gift from God. It was not staged by man, but was a promise fulfilled from Jesus who, in Acts 1:4, told his followers to wait for the coming of the Comforter. And so they waited and obeyed, hoping that whatever was coming would help heal their pain from the loss of Jesus. This happened during the festival of Pentecost, one of three main Jewish celebrations.

Pentecost, which means "fiftieth," is a celebration of the 50th day following Passover. Pentecost is seven weeks of seven days after the day of Passover. This is when the Jews celebrated the harvest (see Lev. 23:15-21).

A small group of Christians were gathered together in one place and in one accord of spiritual achievement, probably celebrating the Jewish Pentecost as they waited on Jesus' promise. Suddenly a divine disturbance in the form of a mighty wind filled the house with such intense power, and there were tongues of fire resting upon all in the room. Everyone was included!

Fire is an amazing phenomenon. It remains in the same condition but for a few seconds. And, in many instances, fire is important. Fire warms that which is cold. It illuminates that which is dark. It purifies that which is impure. It can even duplicate itself by shooting flames to something else.

The Holy Spirit came to earth to empower the people of God so they could become the catalysts of the presence of God in the world. We are now the bridge between Jesus and the Lost. And we are empowered in this work through the presence of the Holy Spirit.

Whatever these "tongues of fire" were, this was an outpouring of God's presence in a mighty and powerful way. And whatever else was happening, suddenly all felt their ability to communicate with one another clarified and heightened. For the first time in their lives this motley mob from a variety of cultures was hearing the Word of God in a way that struck straight to their hearts. Some thought them drunk with wine, but they were not. Peter reminded them, "It's only 9 o'clock in the morning!" This experience was to equip the saints for the next stage in the building of the church. And all were amazed! On Christmas Day we sing "Happy Birthday" to Jesus. On Pentecost we sing "Happy Birthday" to the church.

One other point: Look who is filled with the Spirit and begins to speak—Simon Peter! Now, Peter was known not to be a great orator. And, he was also known for cowardice in his faith, having at several times and places denied being part of Jesus' crew. But here he stands and preaches the first ever-recorded Christian sermon. The Spirit empowered Peter just as we are empowered in ways we can't imagine. And Peter's message: "No matter what has happened, is happening, or will happen, look to Jesus. And from this day forward, *we* are Jesus. We are his witnesses; so repent and be baptized, and let's be church!"

OPPORTUNITIES FOR DAILY LIVING

When the Holy Spirit came into the room of gathered Christians, *no one* was excluded from the gift of the tongues of fire. This gift fell upon everyone: male, female, Jew, Gentile, Egyptian, proselyte, Arab, Roman. All heard the gospel in their own language. All were amazed. Perhaps for the first time in their lives they deeply experienced the inclusive love of God. Until this moment, women had been second-class citizens. Certainly "proselytes, Romans, and Egyptians" would not have previously been welcomed in that gathering. But here they all were.

We have the same opportunity to live this out. *All* are welcomed in the family of God! *All* are included in the saving grace of Jesus. *No one* is excluded!

- What do you love about our church?
- What do you love about the "church universal"?
- What do you think needs to happen to improve our church and God's church?
- What needs to happen to improve your own faith?

God's tongues of fire are here for us too. The fire may be here to warm, illuminate, purify, or to catch something else on fire. What do YOU need? We are the bridge between the earthly ministry of Jesus and the second coming of Jesus.

- What do you need to do to build bridges into the world?
- What does our church need to do to build bridges into the world?
- What words do you need to share?
- For what do you need courage as you build bridges?

PRAYER

God, thank you for *the* church, and thank you for *our* church. We are your people formed in this community. Forgive us when we have been exclusive; forgive us when we have spoken so that some could not understand. Help us to be as illuminating and exciting as the events of that first Pentecost. Help us to "catch fire" and share that fire with the lost among us and around us. Amen.

Preaching in Rome
Acts 28:11-30

OPENING

The church was born in Jerusalem, as we read in the beginning of the Book of Acts. And, as the book comes to a close, we see Paul in the capital of the known world: Rome. At that point the city was home to more than a million people, half of them slaves. A new age had dawned through the outpouring of the Holy Spirit, and Paul had arrived in Rome to continue preaching the gospel message.

Had there been news coverage of the day, many people would no doubt have been following the travelogue to see if indeed Paul would make it to Rome. There were times when he must have wondered to himself, "Lord, is this really what you want of me?"

The strongest of men have weak moments when discouragement, loneliness, and perhaps defeat are at work. How we need each other to keep our spirits up! This poem from Ida Goldsmith Morris is one that keeps me going often:

> It takes so little to make us sad
> Just a slighting word or doubting sneer,
> And our footsteps lag, tho' the goal seems near,
> And, we lose the courage and hope we had.
> So little it takes to make us sad.
>
> Ah, but it takes so little to make us glad,
> A cheering clasp of a friendly hand,
> A word from one who can understand,
> And we finish the task, we long had planned,
> And, we lose the doubt and the fear we had,
> So little it takes to make us glad.

Paul, thanks to some good friends and a few days of rest and recreation among supporters, arrived at Rome. There is something every person can do to inspire and lift up another. Some of you already have this habit. For others of us, let us practice this even more.

OBSERVATIONS ON THE TEXT

After Paul settled in Rome, chained to one of the elite guards of Caesar's palace, he called for the leaders of the Jews to come see him so he could tell them why he was a prisoner. They listened, but typical of men of their day—and even our day too—they only half-listened. They had already made up their minds. So, in verse 28 Paul says that from now on it will be to the Gentiles that he will speak. And they will listen.

Basically, Luke reports, "Okay Jewish people, this is your last chance for a long while." And for two years, at his own expense and still under the guard of Caesar, Paul preached the kingdom of God and the saving grace of Jesus. What looked like an ending was actually a beginning.

Paul stayed in chains under Caesar's orders. We will never know what the interaction may have been between Paul and Caesar. Some believe that in time Paul was acquitted, sent to Spain,

Observations and Opportunities

arrested again, and later executed. Others think Paul was executed by sword in the square of Rome, since he was indeed a Roman citizen. For some reason, Luke, the master of the historical details of the work of the gospel, omits what happened to Paul. Who knows why? Perhaps it was already known to the citizenry of Rome. Perhaps it was just too gruesome or painful to document. And, in the end, the way of death really is not important. What is important is that today Paul's ministry is still at work. Paul's redemption along the Damascus Road not only transformed him, but also transformed the whole world and continues to do so this day. Nothing can stop the victorious words of Christ from thriving.

Sometimes, when it seems that all is lost, we are just on the threshold of a new beginning. We are free to determine *how* we respond to the circumstances around us. Paul continued to find ways to spread the gospel even though he was chained to a Roman guard and imprisoned in Rome. And what happened? The gospel spread! Almost everything had been taken away from this man except his continued faith in Jesus. This is the missionary who told us, "I've learned that in whatever state I find myself to be content. All things work together for good. I preach Jesus the Christ, crucified. The greatest of these is love."

Paul wrote letters to his beloved places of ministry, including 13 books of the New Testament. He sang in jail; he wrote letters (sermons) in jail; he ministered to those around him. And the word of God prospered.

OPPORTUNITIES FOR DAILY LIVING

- Who encourages you, cheers for you, supports you, and affirms you?
- Whom are you encouraging?

You may never know until the other side of heaven what effect your words are having on others. But know that there are those in your life who need you to be their cheerleader and supporter.

Has there ever been a time when you were at the end of your rope? You'd done all you could. You'd invested everything you had to make something happen, and all you could see ahead was failure.

- How has God shown you new beginnings from what looked like failures?
- What has this done for your ability to risk? To encourage others to risk?
- What have you learned about faith?

God rarely gives us the life we think we are going to have. Rarely has my life taken the turns I thought were actually going to happen. But God continues to teach me resilience. I am not where Paul was. I am rarely content in the places I find myself. But I keep praying for God to show me what is next, who is next on my pathway, and what else I can do. What about you?

PRAYER

Forgive us, O God, when we give up too easily. Forgive us, too, when we encourage others to give up too easily. We know that we are a people of faith, and we know that we are called to be faithful. Help us to encourage, to be encouraged, and to continue moving forward in the grace and goodness of Jesus. Amen.

Do all things work together for good?
Romans 8:28

OPENING

The telegram arrived on a Sunday morning at 8:30. It was the middle of World War II and the world was a difficult place. The next action was to call the pastor. "Pastor, we know it's Sunday morning, but we've just received a telegram. Our boy has been killed in action. Can you come?" As pastors do, he dropped everything, made a quick phone call to his associate to let him know he would be at church for worship, and headed to visit with this family. As he drove, he thought of the cold, impersonal, yellowed piece of paper: "We regret to inform you that your son has lost his life in the service of our country. . ." And, he thought even more about what in the world he would say to the family. Words are so empty. And then he prayed, "God, help me to speak rightly; so much depends on what I will say to them." As he entered the room where the couple sat, bleary-eyed from tears, he saw an opened Bible on the table in front of them. "Pastor, if you can, help us to just believe this, that everything is going to be alright." The mother was pointing her finger to Romans 8:28, "We know that all things work together for good for those who love God who are called according to his purpose" (NRSV). They talked and prayed and cried together. When the pastor left, the wife said to her husband, "Everything is going to be alright."

I know it's true, because God's Word tells us this truth. But I can tell you that this is the hardest text in the Bible for me to accept and believe. If we can believe it, we will gain stability in the dark and trying times of life. If we can't believe it, we may find ourselves lost in the darkness of grief and pain for a long while. Let's look at what God is saying to us today and how these verses may help us.

OBSERVATIONS ON THE TEXT

That all things work, we never doubt. Nothing in creation is static; the world is dynamic. Atoms, stars, acorns, dewdrops—everything works together. That's how nature works and how creation works. The sun, the soil, the rain, chemical processes—all work together in cooperation to produce the beauty of God's creation. Everything is working together; one thing leads to another and to another and to another.

Everything works according to a purposeful plan. It appears that when we transfer our thinking from physical to moral and spiritual experiences of life, sometimes we want more explained than we can grasp. We know there are purposes; we just want to know what the purposes are. Rarely, however, do we know the purpose. I've often said to friends, "I can't wait to see how God is going to bring something good out of this!" In the realm of nature we know that night follows day. We know that each part of the natural world plays a role. (I still have some questions about mosquitoes!) But in the spiritual and moral realms there is just so much that we don't know and cannot know. Paul is writing to tell us all, "Everything is going to be okay. Maybe not today, maybe not tomorrow, but sooner or later, everything is going to work out okay."

Great character cannot be developed except through the forging of the joyful and sorrowful. Meaningful people of all times have, without exception, come up through misunderstandings, disappointments, failures, losses, and conflict. Both gold and character are forged and purified in fire. The battle, not the uniform, is what makes the soldier the hero. The qualities of courage and action are not taught in school, but are developed during life, through change and growth.

When God permitted Joseph to be sold into slavery, falsely accused in Potiphar's house, and thrown into prison, God was not exacting punishment on Joseph for some sin. He was weaving into his character qualities for kingship. When God permitted Paul to be thrown into the Roman prison, he was not punishing Paul. He was erecting a monument to the grace of God, demonstrating for all time that God's inner grace is greater than earth's outward circumstances. And, perhaps in our afflictions and heartbreaks, God is working in a purpose just as divine, just as magnificent. So, it is by faith that we accept these incidents as we walk by faith. And we hope that God will one day reveal to us the goodness of what has been happening.

OPPORTUNITIES FOR DAILY LIVING

The untroubled life is not the ideal life. Real happiness comes not from the elimination of trouble, but from the victories that come from the trouble. The sheltered life leads only to loneliness and depression. The victorious life leads us to meaning.

Do we ever get totally beyond a tragedy or trial? No! But we can claim victory over the pain and move on to find even more meaning in our lives.

- What challenges have helped form your character?
- What challenges do you need to rise above?
- What's keeping you from claiming the promise of Romans 8:28?

The things we count as liabilities, God has made into assets. We may not see it, but it is not necessary for us to see—only to believe. We do not judge God's great drama of earth by one isolated incident. The last act is coming and, in that day, all will be made clear. God is working to a greater purpose than any of us can imagine.

- If you could ask God one question, what would you want to know?
- How would knowing the answer to this question help you to be happier or healthier?

The question for most of us is, "Why?" We are better off knowing that God is working for good. We are better off *not* knowing how God is doing that.

The Holy Spirit is at work in our world. We are God's children. We have been born into the spirit of God's love, and God is at work to care for us, even in our trials. The struggles of today are preparing us for the greater moments that are to come. When trials come—and they will—we pray. We take our pain to God. We invite others into our pain to help us carry the burden. And together, God brings to us a new confidence that we *will* overcome the adversity. It is no accident that bad things happen to good people. It is faith at work, knowing that God is behind the struggle and getting us ready for the next great thing. I know this is hard to believe, but I know this is true!

PRAYER

Thank you, God, for the struggles of life. Lord, help my unbelief. The days of life are often so challenging. The days of life are often so confounding. Help me to trust that *you* know the purposes for good. Lord, help my unbelief. Amen.

The superiority of love
1 Corinthians 13:1-7

OPENING

There is nothing that love cannot make better. One of the temptations of the Corinthians was to use their gifts in a self-important manner. They were eloquent in speaking and were quick to tell one another how eloquent they were. They had the gifts of prophecy and were quick to tell each other how much they knew about what was to come. The Corinthians were an arrogant bunch, and they were always trying to outdo one another to prove to others and to God how faithful they were. If you listened to the Corinthians, they were the best Christians in the world—and they were quick to tell you so.

God knows so much more than we do. We think ourselves so superior because we have "book learning" or are people of "letters." But God knows more than all the knowledge of all the books in all the libraries in the world.

God gives without condition. God gives so that we might give. Philanthropy can be carried out for self-glorification—to get one's name on a building or on a wall. Yet, if we give without love, all we get is a plaque on a wall. It is love for Christ and the brethren that makes life worth living. We give not for glory. We give because God gives. We give because God loves!

OBSERVATIONS ON THE TEXT

The Corinthians came from different backgrounds, cultures, temperaments, and outlooks. They were a complicated community. Paul wanted to draw them together into a strong Christian community. This was a strange thing for these people. And so, Paul gave them some basics on how love operates. He described the characteristics of love: patient, kind, and other-centered.

Many of the Corinthians were uncouth or brusque. They said what they thought and didn't worry about where the words fell. Paul tells us to be careful about what we say. Some people are tender, and we have to practice some self-restraint to show love to those around us.

Love that is patient reveals itself in kindness. Kindness seldom costs money, only effort—a smile, a visit to express comfort, a word of encouragement. Kindness is the convincing evidence of Christian love.

Love is never about one's self. Love is always about others. If we are patient and if we are kind, we are focusing on others. Love that is about self is not love. For many of us, these traits seem basic. For the Corinthians, this was new information.

While there are some very positive aspects in how love should operate, there are some attributes that are easier to state in the negative. Paul abruptly shifts to hold the attention of his audience. Love is not jealous, not boastful, not arrogant or rude.

The cause of the first crime in the story of Genesis is jealousy. It strikes deep into life's obvious inequalities. Too many of us are inadequate and try to overcompensate. Jealousy makes this happen. It is selfish to center on one's own self. And jealousy breeds hate and lust. The best way to overcome jealousy is for the Christian to see his neighbor as better than himself.

Jealousy is an inward state of the soul. Boasting is the outward expression of an unchristian spirit. It is sometimes a cover-up for a feeling of inferiority. When a person recognizes and acknowledges his indebtedness to God and to others, he cannot boast about his "self-made" position. We know that all things are from God. Love is indeed modest and humble.

Arrogance is an inner spirit, and rudeness the outward expression. Chapter 11 spoke of how Paul was disturbed by ill-mannered conduct in the church. Those who through arrogance think that what they have to say is so much more important than what someone else says tend to interrupt and be impatient.

OPPORTUNITIES FOR DAILY LIVING

Love bears all things: Wrongdoing is not to be condoned. While love sometimes exposes bad behavior, the cure depends upon our carrying in our hearts a loving attitude toward those who misbehave. This is a form of vicarious suffering where love carries the burden of other's wrongs. Paul knew about this from his former life. Jesus carried Paul's sins on the cross. And so, Paul encourages the Corinthians and us to bear one another up.

Love believes all things: Love is trustful of mankind. To love is to believe in the best and to rouse and evoke the best in men. It can be a challenge and an inspiration for them to live up to. Paul is thinking of the weaker brother in this speech. Let his failings be pointed out, his faults be remedied, but above all let them be made to realize they can recover their place in the community. Those who have been forgiven still have contributions to make. Encourage one another.

Love hopes all things: We go on hoping when there is no ground for hope. There is an authentic ring of personal experience in this with Paul. Christ saw hope in him while Paul was a bitter enemy of the church. Love may not be able to give reasons for its hope, but it keeps on hoping. None of us is worthless. There will always be a chair at the table for the prodigal, hoping against hope that he will return home!

Above all, *love endures all things:* Where there is no obvious ground for faith, we continue to hope and, if hope seems futile, we persevere. At the heart of love is endurance!

PRAYER

Help us to love; help us to hope; help us to endure. But above all, help us to love as you love us. Amen.

Living fully into our calling
Ephesians 1

OPENING

It was not easy to be a Christian in a city like Ephesus. This was a "city of darkness" with lots going on to call one away from a life in Christ. Ephesus was a strategic city for Rome. Like Philippi, there was lots of commerce and diversity. The pull of Rome was very strong here, and so the worship of Caesar and of many other lesser gods was very prevalent here.

Into all this Paul writes a letter of "peace." Paul wrote most of his letters during stress and conflict, but not so with the one to the Ephesians. The mood is one of calm, deep reflection. This is also his least personal letter, which leads us to believe he might have written it to be circulated among the churches of the region.

Perhaps there is a word of calm for us today from our missionary friend, Paul. Let us hear what the Spirit might be saying to the churches.

OBSERVATIONS ON THE TEXT

How one identifies oneself is important. Especially when someone is writing a letter, the identity of the sender is a critical point. Remember that many of the biblical writers identify themselves, not just by name but by reputation and station in life and ministry. One writes to identify wealth or prestige, family or rank. And, so it is with Paul. Note what Paul does.

He identifies himself first as an apostle of Christ Jesus by the will of God. He is not bragging; he is giving glory to God. Many would have known Paul's reputation prior to his conversion. Here he is giving direction of his transformation and glory for the same. His first priority is to serve Christ, and his power source is the will of God.

Imagine Paul sitting in prison, in seclusion, chained to a Roman guard, contemplating all the blessings and gifts God has given to him and to all believers. Among those who need a word is the church at Ephesus, and perhaps even more all the churches of the region. Here is your gift: "Grace and peace from God!" In a city of hustle and bustle, grace and peace seem like wonderful gifts.

God chose the Ephesians before the foundation of the world to be witnesses of Christ. They have been chosen and nurtured and provided for. Where they are in life, in this setting, is not by accident. Is it "predestination"? Some would say "yes," but Paul doesn't use that word. Paul is referring to the culmination of salvation, not the initiation of salvation. God has "hopes" that all of us will be saved. But this is not predestined by a long shot. God still gives us the freedom to choose. Could God "predestine" the story so that it ends with "happily ever after" for everyone? Of course God can, but God won't.

Some things in life we do not choose: our parents, our place of birth, the color of our skin or eyes or hair. But we all have the choice of whether to follow the God who calls us. God has chosen us and sealed the covenant through Jesus. And, God has "predestined" that salvation for all eternity will be the gift for all who call on the name of the Lord Jesus Christ. But again, God gives each of us the choice. Why is this important? Because if we are all predestined to eternal life or eternal damnation, we wouldn't need Jesus and we wouldn't need faith. God has chosen all of us, and he hopes and prays that we all choose him. The Jews were chosen for a reason: to be a light to the Gentiles. The rest of us are chosen to be salt for the world.

We are called to be holy, set apart, different. Just as the temple was a holy building and the Sabbath was a holy day and the priest a holy man, we are called to be a holy people. In today's world we tend to play down the differences. We are better at hiding our lights under bushel baskets. But Paul says that every Christian should be easily identifiable in every aspect of life. And God has made us acceptable to him. We have been redeemed, transformed, and created in the love and grace of Jesus. And what Jesus did was to deliver us from the entanglements of the world that would make us ungodly. The cost of this liberation was very high, and yet many of us still prefer the entangled chaos of living without our Lord.

OPPORTUNITIES FOR DAILY LIVING
- How much are you willing to pay for a gallon of gasoline or a dozen eggs or a gallon of milk?
- How much would you be willing to pay for membership in our church?
- How much would you be willing to pay for your salvation and forgiveness?

God was willing to pay for us with everything (John 3:16-17). God has paid the highest price for our redemption. And yet, many of us still don't believe and many others of us don't obey.

- When you were a child, what did you want your purpose in life to be?
- In your teenage years, what was your hoped-for purpose in life?
- As an adult, what do you think is your purpose?

We live in an age when many people have lost faith that there is any purpose available to them. For many the writer of Ecclesiastes is right: "Everything is futile." But I don't believe that! In complete forgiveness, God gives us the freedom to live more fully in Jesus. There is no secret key to life except to live fully in Christ. This is Paul's message to the churches in and around Ephesus.

Suppose someone who knew nothing about Christianity attended a communion service. It would be to them an unintelligible mystery. There would be little or no meaning to the ritual. In fact, the whole process might seem a bit scary. With all the "eating of body and drinking of blood" language, it would be quite off-putting. But for the Christian, it has very deep meaning.

- What does the Lord's Supper mean to you?
- What do you think it might have meant to the early Christians in Ephesus?

Let us take our understanding and our love of Jesus and go into the world and make a difference. We have the power to take away the mystery! Are we willing?

PRAYER
Give us strength to live the life you wish for us. Give us a clarity of identity that we might be the people you hope us to be. And, give us courage that we might be the disciples you have called us to be. Amen.

98 Lessons for Living

Shining stars
Philippians 2:12-30

OPENING

My Aunt Louise was a writer of some accomplishment. She had at least one book chosen for the "Book of the Month Club." I was privileged to visit her in Connecticut in her little vine-covered cottage nestled near the edge of a cliff overlooking the Atlantic Ocean. She shared with me how ecstatic she was in being permitted to search attics of old homes in the New England area, where she found letters of historical leaders.

So much more is revealed through letters than in formal historical data. In letters we chat with our friends. Paul would be shocked to realize his letters ended up as part of our Holy Scriptures. The letter to the Philippians is perhaps his most personal one, and he surely wouldn't have wanted this one shared. The bond between church and pastor was special, especially between this church and this missionary. In Paul's day Philippi was the largest city in Macedonia, a great crossroads of commercial activity. It was a rich city, a city filled with lots of people, a city strategically placed for doing business.

Philippi had three great claims. In the neighborhood of the city were gold and silver mines. By Paul's day, these mines had run dry, but they had set the tone for the vast wealth in the city. The city had been founded by Philip, father of Alexander the Great. A range of hills and valleys divided Europe from Asia, and only at Philippi was the great crossroad that opened up for transportation—also adding to the city's wealth. Philippi had attained the blessing of being a Roman colony. The community would have been settled by Roman soldiers and their families, also adding to the city's wealth and prestige.

So, we have a rich city with a major trade route between Europe and Asia that was a Roman colony. We have a small Christian church in this city that Paul had planted and personally served for a few years. There is a deeply personal relationship between this church and this man. Just like my aunt's discoveries of personal words, we glimpse some personal interaction.

OBSERVATIONS ON THE TEXT

Paul is writing from prison in Rome. He is probably on his deathbed. He is writing to a congregation and a people he dearly loves. He admonishes the church in verse 12 to "work out your own salvation with fear and trembling." This is not "your salvation comes by works," because Paul does not hold to this. He is calling on the Philippians to work out what God has already started in them. In spite of being a great church, they apparently have a problem within their fellowship. And, they have to work out for themselves what God has already begun. Do *all* things without murmuring and arguing. Claim the innocence. Be blameless.

Strife in a church harms its influence. Paul knows this church has the opportunity to make a difference. The world is a dark place, and a church that shares its light makes a difference. So, Paul is saying to "bring to completion that which we began a long time." God's action cannot be frustrated, nor can it remain half finished. This continuance of the process is dependent upon God. And, the continuance of the process is dependent upon man. God *can* make everything right, but God gives us the freedom to make a choice. What God offers, man must take hold or there is no salvation, no transformation. And that which we do take from God, we take hold of with "fear and trembling." This is not the fear that drives us away from God but that which drives us to God. When we really love God we don't want to hurt/disappoint God, and we move more deeply into God's will.

Paul calls the church to be blameless and happy. In the Christian life we are called to perfection in Christ. We are called to be without blemish. So, Christian purity is to be blameless in the sight of the world and sincere within itself. We offer the world the gospel, and it gives light to the world. Shine like the stars so that the world may know you have influence in your community and in your church.

Paul looks upon the ministry of the Philippians as a libation poured out in sacrifice to the Lord. He reminds them that in the same way he is being poured out, they must be poured out. And, he continues to say "thank you" for the gift they have sent to support his ministry. Epaphroditus, a representative from the Philippian church, brought the gift. It is now time for him to return home and for the Philippians to represent Paul and Christ as models of Christian disciples.

OPPORTUNITIES FOR DAILY LIVING

This was a very small church in a very large city. There were many people with wealth and influence. There were business people, transports, lots of commerce and trading and money. And, there were Roman soldiers everywhere. Paul says to the church, "Remember why we began a church in Philippi. Remember what we started. Now, keep on going, keep on working strategically, intentionally." God calls our churches to do the same. Churches in America have huge opportunity for influence. And, yet, the world sees the worst of us, not the best of us.

What changes do we need to make? How are we to be blameless inside and outside the church? Who taught us how to be church? How are we to live out the model that has been set before us? What are we doing wrong in our churches today? Why are we not representing Jesus as we should?

We need to pray!

In 252 AD a plague broke out in Carthage and people were just throwing the dead out into the streets. People were fleeing the city out of fear of the disease. Cyprian, the Christian bishop of the city, gathered his congregation together for ministry. They buried the dead, nursed the sick, and tended to the city stricken with fear and agony. In doing so, this church saved the city. They risked themselves with reckless courage to serve Christ and neighbor. That is the call of Paul to Philippi and to us. That is the model of Jesus to the world: shining stars for all the world to see that Jesus is Lord of all.

PRAYER

Help us to shine, O God. Forgive us when we choose fear over faith. Forgive us when we are so obsessed with our sinful ways that we forget the joy of our salvation. Help us to be willing to continue the good work you have begun in us. Amen.

The art of living
Philippians 4

OPENING

Sometimes in life we are left with only being able to lift our hands to the sky and cry, "Why me?" In Philippians 4, Paul gives some suggestions on how to live well even in those moments when we ask, "Why me?" Paul is still in prison, his health really deteriorating at this point. Philippi is a rich city, a diverse city, and a strategic Roman colony.

The church has sent a gift to Paul to help with his situation, and he is writing to say "thank you" and express his love and gratitude to them and to challenge them to unity and harmony. His challenge is to stand firm in the love of Jesus. Paul knows that unpleasant relationships, destructive behaviors, negative thinking, worry, and stress are at work in this church and can make life unpleasant. He is concerned that the church be healthy on the inside so that the Christians can be a model of Jesus to the community. In everything rejoice, and this joy can only come from a depth of faith in Jesus.

OBSERVATIONS ON THE TEXT

It is part of our fallen human nature to quarrel. It is ironic that when Christians are in one accord, when they are sincere in their faith, when their beliefs really matter and their enthusiasm is great, that is just when they are most likely to have conflict. Paul is grieved to hear of a quarrel between two women, active workers in the church. Happiness and quarreling cannot coexist in a healthy church. So, with gentle forbearance, determining not to let differences of opinion mar our fellowship, we can learn to live with each other in sweet fellowship. Yet, it is part of our fallen human nature to indulge in impure, negative, and destructive thinking. Paul calls on this church to set aside their differences and get their act together!

Verse 8 is one of the most prolific writings ever on how to live with joy. "Finally, brethren, whatsoever things are true, whatsoever things are honest, whatsoever things are just, whatsoever things are pure, whatsoever things are lovely, whatsoever things are of good report; if there be any virtue, and if there be any praise, think on these things."

First, believe things that are true. There is so much untrue in the world, we have trouble sometimes sorting out what/who to believe. Paul warns, "Follow the truth of Christ." Next, live in honesty. Honesty is noble, just, pure, morally true. Live in the beauty of the world and live virtuously. If we continue to live fully in these good traits of life, we will have the joy of Christ. Paul has taught these people how to live joyfully; he now reminds them to claim that joy.

Paul is in prison and on his deathbed. Yet he is able to talk about the joy of his faith. This joy of faith comes only through right thinking. Living the opposite of verse 8 is *not* right thinking. It is part of our fallen nature to be discontented. If we have little, we want more. If we have a lot, we still want more. The world is falling apart because we are all trying to grab more and more. Paul has learned from his experience how to claim the joy of right thinking. He says to this beloved church, "Here is the key. Be content with what you have!"

Here is another ironic point: The reason we have all these tests is because we have relationships. The very act of caring, hoping, trusting, loving brings us the challenges of daily living. We are in relationship with our neighbors. They get a new car. Suddenly, we are not content. We are in a loving community, and the church down the street has a grand revival. We are not content. We want to be content; it is just not in our nature.

To that end, we have to claim the joy of Christ in our lives. We have to be content, and the *only* way we can claim this joy is in Jesus. Paul lived in a God-sufficiency. We live in a self-sufficiency. We can learn to live into this contentment that Paul speaks about, but only when we live in Jesus.

OPPORTUNITIES FOR DAILY LIVING

We say to ourselves, "I can do everything in life if I believe in myself enough." Paul said, "I can do everything in life through Christ." We have got to quit looking over our shoulders at our neighbors and their stuff. We have got to quit lusting about all the things we don't have. We have got to quit looking the other way when social, moral, and racial injustices are happening.

I'm not saying that we don't have dreams and ambition. I am saying that our dreams and ambition are Christ-centered, not me-centered. So here is the key as Paul stated it: "Be content with what you have!" And here is the key as Jesus stated it: "You shall love the Lord your God with all your heart and all your soul and all your mind . . . and you shall love your neighbor as you love yourself." Now, what's it gonna take for us to make that happen?

When we are so quick to cry, "Why me?" We must be able to also ask, "Why not me?" Where do we get that life is supposed to be fair? If John and I had worried about "fair," we never would have risked our work to form SYSCO. If our church was worried about "fair," we would never reach out beyond our walls for the cause of Christ. Paul was in prison and on his deathbed, but he exclaimed joy and contentment. We live in grand houses, drive great cars, go on wonderful trips, and we still want more. Many of us call this "the American dream." I think we are buying into "the American lie." We have to make some shifts! Now, what's it gonna take for us to make that happen?

We cannot be happy and mad at the same time. And, we cannot be angry with someone while we are praying with them. With whom are you struggling relationally? Take them to dinner and have some good laughs. Go over to their house, take them some cookies, and pray together. Only when we truly begin to love our neighbor as ourselves will we approach the joy of Christ. We have to empty all the negative with the positive so that the good stays in and the bad has no room. Then we can claim joy, contentment, and the love of Jesus. Now, what's it gonna take for us to make that happen?

PRAYER

God, forgive us for our desire for more and more and more. We know in our heads that "more" doesn't make us happy. But sometimes we just can't help ourselves. Help us to want more of *your* good in us so that less of the bad in the world stays out of us. Amen.

No fear!
2 Timothy 1:7

OPENING

The following was carved in the mantel of an old house in the suburbs of London: "Fear knocked at the door. Faith answered. No one was there!"

There is a sense in which fear is a defense mechanism. But most of the time when we feel scared, this comes not from the outside to the inside, but is created from the inside and moves outward. We hear a bump in the night and think someone has broken into our home. We get some bad news and go immediately to the worst-case scenario. We get a call from the bank or the doctor and think the worst is about to happen. We are our own worst enemies where fear is concerned. Experiences of fear are usually of our own making. We react with fear to an event rather than an event itself being a truly fearful one.

For many people, fear is a central problem of life. We fear the unknown. We fear the dark. We fear that we are inadequate. We fear our opinions are wrong. We fear that others have an unfavorable opinion of us. We fear old age, poverty, and loneliness. Some people just live fearfully! Fear incapacitates, saps strength, paralyzes, and is a mark of self-centeredness and inner weakness. But God tells us over and over again, "Fear not!"

OBSERVATIONS ON THE TEXT

Paul wrote to Timothy, telling him not to fear. With all the hostility that surrounded Timothy, it is quite understandable that he might have fears. It could have been physical fears. Every time he heard the tread of the marching feet of Roman soldiers, did he think of prison? Certainly, his mentor Paul was in prison. Or, did he think of Jesus, knowing that other soldiers had crucified his Lord? Or, perhaps he was paralyzed by a fear of failure. He who will not risk failure will never know the joy of victory.

Paul listed for Timothy the marks of courage for facing fear: power, love, and self-control. These come from the continuing presence of life in Christ.

Power is not leadership power, but a power over fear. God gives us the power to cope, to overcome our fears. In Christ we have the power to stand in the face of shattering situations and overcome them. In soul-searing situations and wounding disappointments we have the power to hold on to our strong faith. We have the power in Christ to meet life adequately and to keep moving forward.

First John 4:18 gives us the perfect contrast between love and fear: "There is no fear in love. Perfect love casts out fear!" How does this happen? When I love, I am no longer the chief object of my thoughts. Fear turns the doors of my heart inward. The focus is on myself; my soul is narrowed, and it contracts. Love turns the doors of my heart outward. The focus is on another; my soul broadens and expands. Fear nurtures an unhealthy self-consciousness and places self on the throne, fearing it will be deposed. Let's get our eyes off ourselves. Our security rests not on our faith or our fears, but on the *object* of our faith and the *origin* of love. God is trustworthy to overcome our fears.

A sound mind with self-discipline casts out fear. Sober good sense and a reasoned disciplined mind will lead to a well-ordered life. Control of one's self will keep us from panic and fear. We know from past experiences that fear rarely wins. A sound mind reminds us, "You survived the last time this happened. God was with you then, and God will be with you now."

Timothy certainly needed to be reminded of this. If Paul, who was in prison, could say, "Fear not," then certainly young Timothy could claim this too—and so should we! The purpose of this letter from Paul was to put heart and confidence in Timothy. There is no greater inspiration than to feel that someone believes in you. Fear makes us feel "in-fear-ior"—and leaders must not feel that. Paul encouraged and moved Timothy toward remembering the strength of Christ that was within him. He reminded young Timothy to "rekindle the gift" of his calling. I can almost hear Paul saying, "Restore the joy of thy salvation" (Ps. 51:12) to young Timothy.

Paul knew what it was like to have "fair weather" friends and to have "bracing" friends. In verses 15-18 Paul reminds Timothy of some of these. And Paul reminds Timothy, "I am a bracing friend to you, so fear not!" Joy of joys is to have friends who care for us and stand with us in troubling times. Paul was such a friend to Timothy.

OPPORTUNITIES FOR DAILY LIVING

Every one of us can be a bracing friend to someone. This strong, supportive kind of friendship should be our nature. Bracing friends look for people to prop up. Bracing friends have a clear purpose and a firm faith. Bracing friends have spiritual reserves with a contagious enthusiasm for the Lord that cannot be contained.

- Who needs you to be a bracing friend to them?
- Who is your bracing friend?

All who stand for the gospel will eventually suffer for the Lord's sake. Remember the beatitude: "When persecuted for righteousness sake, you are blessed. You will inherit the kingdom of heaven" (Matt. 5:10). Paul knew this to be true; so do we. And when we suffer for the gospel we can claim the power, love, and self-control of which Paul wrote.

- Which do you need more in your life: power, love, or self-control? Why?
- How can you claim these alternatives to fear in your life?

Joy of joys, we don't have to earn God's power. It is all part of God's grace. Paul's confidence in God was unflagging. So, too, must ours be.

PRAYER

Even when I walk through dark valleys, please help me, O God, not to have fear. Help me to claim your power, your love, and your self-control to be my strength. Thank you for the continued goodness with which you guide me. I can do all things through Christ. Thanks be to God! Amen.

Inspiration of the Bible
2 Timothy 5:16

OPENING

The Bible is God-inspired and God-preserved. The Bible is a book of encouragement, instruction, inspiration, and direction, and a historical record of the people of God in their interactions with God and one another.

There are three views of inspiration: liberal, fundamentalist, and inspired truth.

According to the liberal view, in the same sense that any author produces his best work, the biblical writers sat down, gave their thoughts, and the work emerged. This puts the Bible on the same level as any other work of literature such as the works of Shakespeare or Milton or even modern-day writers of fiction and non-fiction. One danger here is that the Bible is useless to the larger body of readers.

According to the fundamentalist view, the biblical writers sat down and God dictated word by word, comma by comma, even to the spelling of every word. This view takes the personality and even the life experiences out of the process. One danger here is that the Bible becomes an idol and is elevated to the level of the Trinity.

In the same sense of the liberal view, those who believe in the Bible as inspired truth believe the biblical writers sat down with a collection of ideas and life experiences and then God guided their ideas and they formed a body of work communicating the truth of God. The writers were conscious of God's leadership and that a force "outside of themselves" was leading, but they did not lose their ability to interpret experiences in their own personalities.

So, let's think about these ideas today and hear what Paul is saying to Timothy and to us about the truth of the Bible.

OBSERVATIONS ON THE TEXT

We have no original manuscripts to help us have the "literal autographs" of the writings. But we know that ancient people were careful to guard the documents they possessed. We have abundant evidence that the "scrolls" were carefully copied and carefully kept. The original thoughts were preserved as best as ancient people could.

The Bible we have now was completed about 400 AD, though we think the actual books were written by 40 men between 1400 BC and 100 AD. Long, careful, and prayerful gatherings studied each book that has been included into the official "canon" of Scripture. The 66 books we have (the Catholic Bible has 73 books) were approved by official councils that agreed upon each book attesting to one main theme: the interaction of God with God's people. Each council would look to maintain consistency of thought and story, and the manuscripts were fairly easy to control for consistency until the invention of the printing press by Gutenberg about 1440 AD.

The Bible is the first to share an idea of righteousness as a part of religion. Other faith groups worshipped many gods, idols, icons—all of which were made in the image of man. Christianity says, "NO! We are made in the image of God, the Jehovah God, the one and all-powerful, all-knowing God. Anything God does is right because God is moving toward the ultimate redemption of the world. And, no matter how cruel or unfair the actions of God may seem, God is the ultimate judge of how these factor into the journey towards eternity."

This last part has been a hard thought for many people to accept. Why would a God of love destroy nations while allowing terrible evil to exist in other parts of the world? This is indeed what makes the role of faith so important. Either we trust that we accept God and what God is doing, or we don't trust God. Either we accept Jesus as God's son to lead us to eternal life, or we don't.

But hear what Paul said to young Timothy, "ALL scripture is inspired by God and is useful for teaching, for reproof, for correction, and for training in righteousness." That is a powerful affirmation of a book of collected writings. And, Paul said all this before the canon had been formed. He was basically referring to the Old Testament and saying, "We can depend on God to do only that which is right for *all* the world."

Originally, all that would become scripture was oral. The tradition of God was stories shared among families and passed from generation to generation. While the stories were carefully kept, you know how stories get "reinterpreted" sometimes around your family. While the same could be true in these biblical stories, we trust that the Holy Spirit was guiding the storytelling. Then the stories were written on clay tablets, actual fragments of which have been discovered through the years. Then the stories were written on papyrus (a simple form of paper); some fragments of these have been discovered as well, the most famous being the Dead Sea Scrolls. In 1604 King James asked for a new translation of Scripture. He appointed 54 scholars who took seven years to bring a new and perhaps most accurate translation up to that time.

OPPORTUNITIES FOR DAILY LIVING

For thousands of years the Holy Scriptures were kept from the masses. Only priests or other extremely educated religious scholars were allowed access. Why? Well, one way to control the masses was to quote Scripture as "law" to them. Since they didn't know the true Scripture, the law could be misused for power and control. Jesus fought about this.

Some of this is going on in the world today now. We have to meditate on the Word daily to let its truth permeate us and lead us as righteous disciples of Jesus. How much time are you spending in God's Word, letting the truth of Scripture form you?

There may seem to be contradictions in Scripture verses. For sure there are passages that aren't as clearly stated as they might be. The ambiguity of the Bible has caused holy wars. That same ambiguity is causing major disagreements among good and righteous people today. So, how do we live in the truth of the Bible? We live as people of faith focused on the words of Jesus. At any point where there is ambiguity or disagreement, we look to our Lord.

PRAYER

Thank you, God, for your holy word. There is much about you and your Bible that we don't understand. Help us to live in faith and continue using this lamp to our path and light of our life that we may continue to be your disciples.

The call of God
Mark 1:16–2:17

OPENING

Often, getting started is the hardest part of any job. Once we get in the flow of the work, the processes begin to identify themselves and the work seems to just "happen." And, so it was with the ministry of Jesus. While he had an extra "edge" perhaps, Jesus still had things to do to get his ministry in gear.

For instance, he had to decide what his main message was going to be. This was pretty much decided in his coming to earth, but there was still work to be done. He had to figure out where his ministry would be, how he would finance the work, and what his staff was going to look like. Now, Jesus knew the larger vision, but as a fully human itinerant preacher, he still had to pick folks and put processes in place to help the ministry succeed.

Jesus had eyes of faith, and his heart was attuned closely to God's heart. He was able to see and discern with lots more clarity than most of us. Perhaps if we were to attune our hearts closer to God, we might have similar wisdom. Jesus saw talent. He saw ability. And he was able to look deeply into the hearts of those whom he called.

Can you hear the call of Jesus today? God is still calling us into service. Perhaps we might hear a new call, a fresh call today as we examine these chapters.

OBSERVATIONS ON THE TEXT

Jesus chose ordinary people who were already occupied in their vocations to work with him. What eyes Jesus had! The choosing of Simon and Andrew was not just happenstance. Jesus had walked by this shore many times. He saw the many fishing boats that would have been out on the Sea of Galilee. He saw who were accomplished fishermen and who were not. He saw the work ethic and the passion of the fishermen. And he saw even more: Jesus saw their potential—potential for impacting the Kingdom of God.

And as he walked a little farther down the road, Jesus saw James and John, the "sons of thunder." No, they were not a pro wrestling tandem nor batters for the Astros; these were indeed men of passion. They were also good at fishing. They were brought up in the "family business," and they dropped their nets and followed.

God calls people who are open to the call. They are not idly sitting waiting on some supernatural experience. They are not usually in the church on Sunday or in the holy of holies on the Sabbath. Those called are not in some secret hiding place practicing their Greek or Hebrew. God calls followers who are busy, concerned, passionate, and willing to be disciples.

Notice too that Jesus did not say: "I have a wonderful theological system that I would like for you to investigate. We have similar beliefs that I think will make for a wonderful team." He didn't even say: "Here is the contract. Go home and think it over, pass it through your lawyer, and make sure the terms are agreeable. Talk it over with your spouse and your family, and then let me know." No! Jesus said, "Follow me!" This was a personal calling, and the responses were immediate. Jesus saw something in them. They saw something in him. And they joined forces!

Now, look also at where Jesus went and what he did. There was no professional ministry in the synagogue. The ruler of the synagogue simply called on someone competent to read from the Torah and give "a lesson." These were usually the scribes, the experts in the law. It was their profession to translate interpretations of the law to form faithful people of God. These lessons would usually begin with, "There is a law . . .," and then they would interpret.

Jesus, however, would teach with personal authority. Jesus would begin with "You have heard it said . . . but I say to you . . ." His was an authority he claimed from God, not from the law. When Jesus spoke, he didn't quote scholars on the law; he spoke in the finality of God. And the people were amazed. He spoke and ministered to the needs of the people. And the people were amazed. He spoke as one who not only knew the law, but also lived the law. And the people were amazed!

OPPORTUNITIES FOR DAILY LIVING
- How has God called you?
- Has God called you by name?
- Has God called you out during a revival meeting or a youth camp?
- Why has God called you?
- Have you been called to be "fishers of men" or to other purposes?
- How have you responded?
- Have you given an immediate response, or are you still "praying about it"?

My prayer is that we are all ready when Jesus calls, that we are all sharing daily our love of Jesus.

- How does Jesus amaze you?
- Have you been sick and then made well?
- Have you been lost but now are found?
- Have you been thinking/praying about something, only to have God answer your prayer?

Life in Christ is amazing. Just as God called those ordinary men of old, God is still calling us today—men and women. I stand amazed in the presence of Jesus!

PRAYER
How marvelous! How wonderful! And my song shall ever be. How marvelous! How wonderful! Is my Savior's love for me! Thank you, God, for being so amazing. Help me to respond with passion and intentionality when I hear you calling me. Amen.

The mystery of mysteries
Revelation 1

OPENING

There are people who brag about knowing everything there is to know about the book of Revelation. This is the most mysterious of all mysteries in the Bible. Now, I love a good mystery. But, I already know how this one turns out. While many people avoid looking into this book, there are great words of affirmation and comfort in it.

In the midst of the mystery is not only affirmation and comfort; there is an inspiriting and enduring truth. The truth of this Revelation to John opens the curtains of history to enable us to see what happens to humanity and how the human story ends. It is a perfect ending.

We come to this final book and see the word "revelation" or "apocalypse." The apocalypse is the unveiling or revealing of what is to come. For many people, this is the most difficult book in the Bible to understand. It is also the most avoided book of the Bible for many and may be the most misinterpreted book.

So, today, let's look at this opening chapter to get an insight into the mystery.

OBSERVATIONS ON THE TEXT

The purpose of this book is to reveal the Living Christ, last seen as he ascended into heaven. The attention centers on the person of the book and the people of the book. While there are many codes and symbols, and while the "key" to understanding these may have been lost to us, the Christian community would have understood the meanings and gained comfort.

Rome was the great dragon, the anti-Christ. And in the end, the dragon is slain by the Christ. The people of John's day would have been acquainted with the symbolism, and gained great comfort knowing that at some point their domination by Rome would end and that evil would be defeated once and for all.

There are three ways of looking at Revelation for interpretive purposes: amillenial, premillennial, and dispensational premillennial. Regardless of how complex or simple you may see what God is going to do, it won't matter. I will leave the time and how of God's return to God. What most interests me is what the writer was trying to say clearly to his people. And clearly, John, an apostle of Jesus, loved the Christians of his day and wanted to assure them of God's love for them. While an apostle, at this point he calls himself a prophet. When he mentions the apostles, he refers to them as the 12 foundations of the church. Again, scholars disagree on whether this was John the apostle or not. Regardless of who the author was, these things we know: He was a Christian, he lived in Asia, and he identified as a brother in Christ. He understood his audience, he had great feeling for his audience, and he knew that Christ was returning with love and victory.

Gradually the worship of Caesar had become the universal religion of the Roman empire. The profession of faith was, "Caesar is my lord!" Anyone under the rule of the empire could at any point be stopped and ordered to profess loyalty to Caesar. Domitian, the ruler of Rome at this point, had a less-than-stellar pedigree for the throne, so he ruled by serious violence and intimidation. He was intolerant of any religion other than Caesar religion. He claimed himself to be divine. During Domitian's reign, loyalty was not a test; it was a requirement. If you refused to honor Domitian with "Caesar is my lord," then you could be put to death on the spot.

Christians were put in danger because of their profession of faith, "Jesus is my Lord!" No true Christian would proclaim the title of Lord to anyone but Jesus, which infuriated Domitian and made his violence upon the Christian community even more horrible than on other groups.

John's commission was written to the Christian community to give support and remind all that *no one* is God except God; that *no one* is more powerful than Jehovah God!

Here are a few symbols that are helpful in the writing:

<u>7</u> is the complete number, the divine number. When John said he was writing to the 7 churches, he meant that he was writing to every church—the complete Christian community.

<u>3</u> always relates to the Triune God: God the Creator, Jesus the Savior, and the Holy Spirit.

<u>4</u> usually relates to humankind and the world. The four seasons, the four directions—all relate to the world.

<u>7</u> candlesticks probably represent the 7 churches of Asia Minor to whom John was writing.

The vision of Christ is more powerful, more brilliant, and more beautiful than any statue of Caesar that might be on display.

OPPORTUNITIES FOR DAILY LIVING
- What do you fear?
- What is a symbol that this fear might could represent?

Is there anything in the world that Christ can't overcome? The answer is NO! John was writing to say that Christ is more powerful than anything on earth. This is why this revelation came to John: to encourage those whom he cared about. We need people in our life to encourage us.

- Who encourages you? How?
- Whom do you encourage? How?

John used a secret code for his good friends. He wanted the whole Christian world to know that Jesus the Christ was more powerful than "the dragon" code word for Caesar!

- Who was your best friend when you were a child or a teenager?
- Did you have secrets that just the two of you shared?
- Did you have inside jokes or secret code words with one another?

The Lamb comes with a two-edged sword. This is one of the more powerful weapons of its time. The word of God is powerful, and one symbol for that power is this sword.

- What is a symbol for your power?
- How can you claim the power of God in your life even more?

Prayer
God, the little bit that we understand about you is about the size of a grain of sand or a mustard seed. And you have promised that if our faith is just this size, we can move mountains. Help us to claim your power as our power in our "mustard seed" faith today! Amen.

The call to give*
2 Corinthians 8:1-15

OPENING

Money is unimportant! We need it only if we never die. Money talks, so they say, but the only word it knows is "goodbye." I've noticed that my money doesn't talk at all; it just goes away without saying anything.

Our world seems obsessed with *getting*. We are not so much concerned about *giving*. The grace of giving has to be developed. Giving is a choice; it is a moment of worship; it is a response to the loving God.

Mr. and Mrs. Fleming of Fort Worth struck oil in 1919. While others jumped for joy when the first well came in, Mr. Fleming quietly went into a tool shed, fell on his knees and prayed, "Dear Lord, don't let this make a fool out of me." The Flemings gave more than $20,000,000 to Christian causes during their lifetimes.

Giving can never be a joyful experience until it is regarded as a privilege, not a duty. The heart must precede the hand if joy is to result. I really enjoy writing my check to the church each week, but I have not always enjoyed it. I've had to grow into this joy. I've had to trust in myself, in John, and in God. I've learned that Christian stewardship is an attitude, not a mathematical formula. It is a deeply personal choice.

OBSERVATIONS ON THE TEXT

Deuteronomy 15:7-6 and 10-11 lay down our duty of generosity: "Do not be hard-hearted or tight-fisted toward your needy neighbor. Give liberally and be ungrudging." Too many of us give liberally, but we begrudge the gift.

The New Testament also reminds us of the principles of giving. We are reminded that the joy of giving beyond our means is for good purposes. Giving is a joy, so give willingly; it is a blessing. It is a bit like sowing seeds. If the giving is sparse, the crop will be sparing. If it is generous, the crop will be overflowing.

We cannot walk through the pages of the Bible without stepping all over some aspect of material giving. Jesus talked more about money than about any other subject. We are called to be generous Christians.

Not many people in this congregation remember the Great Depression of the 1930s, but I do. Coca-Colas were a nickel each, and hamburgers a dime. I was a teenager during those years, and I received a whole 50 cents a week to spend in any way I chose. I had been taught that the Bible says we owe 10 percent of all that came into our possession to the Lord, so every week one nickel went into my offering envelope.

My father, not wanting his children to think God only accepted nickels and dimes, gave each of his five children one dollar a week of his own tithe to put into our envelopes. It seemed like a lot of money to me but, of course, it was not under our control. It was a great lesson in generosity and what it means to give beyond one's means. This is a picture of how the Macedonians gave to Paul.

At age 16 I got my first job: working in a doctor's office for $55 a month. It was as natural for me to tithe that money as it was for me to put my shoes on to go to church. There was no decision to be made. By that time in my Christian journey, it was simply my way of life.

Observations and Opportunities

Whenever I think of tithing now, I smile on the inside. In tithing, I knew there was at least one thing I was doing that God expected me to do.

The apostle Paul was smiling when he received the love gift from the churches of Macedonia. He called upon the churches at Corinth to be as generous as the Macedonian churches were. Paul challenged the Corinthians at several points:

Be liberal in your giving. Abound in everything; see that you abound also in this.

Be glad in your giving. Everyone should give accordingly and not grudgingly.

Be faithful in your giving. God requires stewardship; may we be found faithful.

OPPORTUNITIES FOR DAILY LIVING
- If you are a tither, what or who convinced you to tithe? When?
- Does prosperity make giving easier or harder? Why?
- How do you want to be remembered by your family, your friends, your church?

There are many ways to give, and all of us can be and need to be good givers.

We give of ourselves when we give gifts of the *heart*. We give love, kindness, joy, forgiveness, sympathy, and grace.

We give of ourselves when we give gifts of our *minds*. We share ideas, dreams, purposes, principles and inspiration.

We give of ourselves when we give gifts of our *time*. We share interest in others, we sit with those who are struggling, and we give beyond our own selfish motives.

We give of ourselves when we give gifts of our *words*. We share encouragement, comfort, cheer, and guidance.

We give of ourselves when we give gifts of our *money*. It is a joy to give. Since my heart experienced the joy from God for my gifts, I have wanted to give more and more.

- How is your giving?
- How can you give more?

The Macedonians were an example to the Corinthians and to other churches. Paul desperately needed support to continue his missionary work.

- Have you ever been an example to someone?
- What do you think Paul expected of the Corinthians?
- What do you think Paul would say in a letter to you today?
- How can you respond like the Macedonians?

PRAYER

Help me, God, to be a generous person. Help me give to further the missionary movement. Help me give to help those who so desperately need a hand up. Help me give that you may restore the joy of my salvation. Thank you for the joy of giving generously to your work. Amen.

*This lesson and the next three reflect the boldness and commitment of Eula Mae Baugh to her church through tithing.

The focus of giving
Malachi 2:17–3:12

OPENING

The subject of tithes and offerings can be a real test of one's loyalty. Giving is a way to certify that one's faith is genuine. The tithe was not to be the second, fourth or last tenth of our possessions, but the first.

When expenses increase without any increase in income, the Lord's cause seems to be the first to suffer. Why? Is it because he doesn't send us a bill? Did you realize that the Lord's work here is supported by only one third of our congregation? Why?

Jesus said, "Where your treasure is, there will be your heart also." Does this mean that wherever I place the priority of money, my heart will be in that priority? Do you believe that if God has your resources, he has you?

The call to bring the full tithe unto God is a positive command. If we choose to ignore it, do you think God notices? "Test me!" is what God says through Malachi. Let's hear the challenge from this prophet.

OBSERVATIONS ON THE TEXT

Abraham gave a tithe both of political and religious significance. This example extended into New Testament times, as we see in Hebrews 7:2 and 4. Abraham knew that the Lord would take his gift and use it in many good ways.

In New Testament times, tithing was an orthodox procedure among the Pharisees (Luke 18:12). Jesus chided them for their minute exactness in contrast to the more important virtues of justice, mercy, and faith (Matt. 23:23). He also taught his followers that the tithe was binding on the Jews of his day as much as it had been required by Old Testament law. The doom brought upon the rich man of Luke 12 was in part due to his lack of giving as an acknowledgement of God's ownership of everything and of man's stewardship.

Two statements here weary God because they were not honest questions, but cynical accusations. God does not love evil; God is patient with evil with hope for redemption. God's justice comes in God's own time, not when we say. God is a refiner, separating the good from the bad, the gold and silver from the dross. Who can withstand this refining? It is only those who are faithful to God through Jesus Christ. Mature Christians will endure the refining, for they have made a commitment to give and have set aside their first gifts rather than giving God only their leftovers.

There is a relationship between faith and right giving. The people in Malachi's time concluded that God was morally indifferent to their way of life. Throughout history, people have noted that God often seems to treat the wicked more favorably than he does the righteous. But the Bible is very clear: The wicked do seem to prosper, not because God is morally indifferent but because God is redemptively patient. Divine justice comes—on God's timetable and not ours. The question Malachi confronts is "Why should I give tithes and offerings to God if the blessings are the same whether I give them or not?" Malachi's audience was more concerned about what they could get from God than about what they could give out of grateful hearts.

Verse 8 tells us, "You have robbed me in your tithes and offerings." A businessman was complaining to his pastor during his church's pledge drive, "I don't know what people expect

Observations and Opportunities

of me. I can't tithe because I don't know what my income is going to be this year." His pastor replied, "You can write us one big check at the end of the year!" There is no excuse for not tithing.

Tithing was a practice long before the law was established. Abraham and Jacob were tithers. Tithing is clearly supported by the farmers, the businessmen, the political leaders. Everything we have is the Lord's. We are to tithe as an act of worship. When we refuse to return to God a portion of what is rightfully his, we rob God. When we give generously, we are worshipping God and acknowledging to ourselves that all we have is God's.

"Put me to the test," says the Lord of Hosts (v. 10). God is challenging the Israelites. Bring everything to the storehouse and see what happens! While the Bible warns against putting God to the test, here God challenges the people. God is trying to fan the flames of devotion in this sinful nation. The people are indifferent to God, sinful, skeptical. Sound familiar? God was trying to reach this lost people. God promised Malachi's people that if they trusted him, the windows of heaven would be thrown open and blessings would overflow.

OPPORTUNITIES FOR DAILY LIVING

We do not give to get; we give because we have already received more than we deserve. And, as we receive more, we are to give more. And, as we give more and more, we grow in gratitude to God and in contentment with what we have received from God. Many people give God only their leftovers.

- What has God given you?
- What have you given to God?
- What is your testimony of your experience of tithing?

We give until it hurts, and then we give until it stops hurting. Giving and tithing are privileges. Tithing is the blessing of seeing God glorified through the human needs that are met through our giving. Often, by daring to tithe, our faith is renewed. The greatest blessings of my faith are when I have satisfying relationships with other people and with God. My tithing allows each of these relationships to prosper.

- How much would you have to give for it to hurt?
- How much would you have to give for it to stop hurting?
- How can giving money to God's work help you be more focused on the needs of the world instead of your own needs?

Jesus said that where your treasure is, there your heart will be also.

- How do you keep your money from controlling your heart?
- How do you keep a right relationship between your heart and your treasures?

PRAYER

Lord, I need to be a better giver. Help me to give and to be disciplined enough to give generously. Help me to give and to be thankful enough to give generously. Help me to give, to be generous enough to give worshipfully. Help me to give. Amen.

The miracle of giving
Exodus 35–40

OPENING

It is astounding and no less the miraculous working of God that we should be studying lessons right now that parallel the experiences through which our church is going. We are in the middle of a challenging opportunity to make a great and daring move to greater service. We are pledging a new building for a house of worship that will be a tabernacle sufficient and pleasing to God.

Moses, too, was in the middle of a crisis that required a great and daring move. Imagine the task of moving more than 600,000 adult men and their belongings PLUS all the women, children, and animals connected to them with only a three-day supply of food. With all the difficulties involved in this, God told the people to build and furnish a tabernacle for worship that would be moved from place to place! God ordered not only worship, but also the plan and method of worship. The need for worship was declared by God with the expressions of worship placed on the leaders. The same is still true today. Let's think on these things together.

OBSERVATIONS ON THE TEXT

The purpose of worship: God said that his people were to take the time to worship. Wherever they were and whatever they were doing, they were to stop and worship. A place for worship is important. The time for worship is the Sabbath. We are called to keep this day holy. In Moses' day there was a severe penalty for not doing so. The Sabbath was to bring the people's minds and hearts together to focus on God. Worship was for focusing on God. Worship was for focusing on the community of God's people. The same is true for us today. A new place of worship for us will be a wonderful tabernacle in which to focus on God and to deepen relationships with one another.

The place of worship: The tabernacle was to have three compartments: a courtyard, a holy gathering place, and a holy of holies. The people were to gather for worship in the courtyard. The priests were to worship in the gathering place, and the high priest would be permitted into the holy of holies once a year. The holy of holies was to remind all the people and the priests that there is a distance between man and God. Man is in sin and is not to have direct access to God. Even the high priest could not enter the holy of holies without making a blood atonement. How grateful we should be that we have direct access to God even in our sinful nature! God's grace is sufficient to allow us to experience even deeper, more holy worship.

The posture of worship: Only when we draw near to God in worship through the blood of Jesus Christ and stand in his righteousness is our worship acceptable. Trying to worship God in any other manner is blasphemy. We cannot worship God based on our own merits. We cannot worship God based on our good intentions. We cannot worship God based on the good name of a family member. We can only truly worship God in our own salvation. However, Jesus is our high priest. Jesus was made a blood atonement for us. Because of him and his sacrifice, we all are invited in to worship, to grow closer to God and closer to one another.

The provision for the place of worship: The miracle of giving to build a house of worship stirs hearts. When we give to the glory of God, we are moved in ways we have never thought of. We are to pledge for our new building in the same way—to glorify God. The miracle of giving is also that when our hearts are stirred, our spirits become more unified and more willing. A stirred heart is always followed by a more willing spirit. And as our spirits become more willing, we are able to give even more for God's glory. Consider the experience that our "Big Gifts Committee" has had in pledging our new building. One family has pledged their farmland for this new tabernacle. Several have given large pieces of jewelry. If you believe in something, you will support it. Just as Moses and his people supported the building of their tabernacle, so are we supporting our new place of worship.

There's one last thing for us to see today. In Exodus 35:22 we note that the gifts of the women were interesting. Their gifts were not equal to the gifts of the men. Women did not have property. Women did not have money. They were at the mercy of their husbands. However, the women did have valuables to give. They had time and skills; they had jewelry and rings; they had rich fabrics and yarn. They gave as fully as the men did. We are answerable to God about how we obtain our possessions and what we do with our possessions. The women gave sacrificially. In fact, Exodus 36:6-7 tells us that they received so much in offerings that Moses told them to quit giving! (That would never happen in a Baptist church!) God always takes our gifts and multiplies those gifts, blessing the gift and the giver with his approval.

OPPORTUNITIES FOR DAILY LIVING

How can it be that we are studying these lessons on giving at the same time we are pledging for our new building? This is another evidence of the miracles of God and the miracles of giving.

- How is God amazing you?
- How are you responding to the astounding work of God's Spirit?

Are women and men not equal? In biblical days women were nothing more than possessions. When Moses called the people to give, men and women were in line to give. All came with a willing heart. The women gave as much as the men. This is something for us to see in our church too.

- Women, what can you give to our new work?
- Would you willingly give up your gold and jewelry?

A rich man remarked to another passenger on the train as they were passing a big church building, "If people would stop building these big churches and give to the poor, it would make a bigger impression." The other passenger showed his clerical collar and, to the amazement of the rich man, responded, "Yes, I've heard that before." The rich man was proud, and said, "I'm so glad you agree. From whom have you heard this?" "Judas Iscariot!" replied the cleric.

We cannot let our pride get in the way of our giving. We cannot let smaller visions get in the way of larger visions.

- What are you doing to make ready our new tabernacle?

PRAYER

Lord, not all of us can give a large farm or portions of gold. Some of us cannot even give much money. But we can all give something—be it our money, our possessions, our time, or our talents. Impress upon us, O God, what we can give so that we too can be participants in the miracle of giving. Amen.

The accountability of giving
Matthew 25:14-30

OPENING

We know that to whomsoever much is given, much is required. Does this apply only to those endowed with spiritual knowledge and insight or also to those in places of leadership or financial strength?

Well, today I am living out this requirement. I would have preferred to be assigned a lesson to discuss something like, "Love thy neighbor" or "How to be a good husband or wife." But no! This is today's assignment, so here goes.

The situation in today's lesson takes place after Jesus' triumphal entry into Jerusalem. Jesus sat at the Mount of Olives, just two days before the feast of the Passover when he would be betrayed. He had left the temple with scathing denunciation of the scribes and Pharisees. He had wept over Jerusalem. And now, in an intimate conversation with his disciples, he is talking about things to come. So today, Jesus talks to us.

OBSERVATIONS ON THE TEXT

In Matthew 25:14-30 we see a man summon his servants and tell them to take care of his land. (This story is also found in Luke 19 and referenced in 1 Peter 4:10.) "As every man has received the gift, even so minister the same as good stewards of the manifold grace of God." Sometimes we forget that we aren't independent entities. Some of us believe, like the Pharisees, that we are the landowners and the elite. We are not! God can drop us if he chooses. Stewardship is not about our giving God some money. Stewardship is about God using us and our money to glorify him and expand his ministry.

As recorded in Matthew 25:15, the landowner gives out a variety of gifts. In 1 Corinthians 12 there is a list of gifts, with not one of them being ranked above another in importance. These gifts were given over and above the normal care for the servants. They were not given as rewards; they were given for investment. They were to be traded to expand the owner's property. Trading was a way of life in New Testament times. Jesus' audience would certainly have been familiar with what the owner was doing. These are all investments that the owner expected them to use to expand his properties. Some did really well and were rewarded. One did nothing, and he too was rewarded—but in a bad way. We are to use the gifts God has given us to expand his kingdom. God expects us to take our gifts, invest them, and expand his realm and ministries.

What does it mean to be faithful with what one has been given (Matt. 25:20-30)? Just as each servant was judged in the same way for the same thing—his effort—God requires the same of us.

Our judgment of human worth is based mostly on false standards, standards that waste a lot of our lives and standards that see us trying to impress each other with our wealth, our intellect, or our power. None of these mean a thing. The owner of the property set three standards and applied these equally to each servant: effort, ability, opportunities for work. Of these, only effort is under our control. We are responsible for the quality and extent of our effort. We are to do the best we can with what we have. We are not responsible for our inborn ability. We are not responsible for the opportunities that may or may not come our way. We are responsible for our effort, for improving ourselves and those for whom we work. When we make full use of our effort to enhance our abilities and opportunities, we are faithful stewards.

Observations and Opportunities

- How much effort are you putting into your giving to our church, to God's church?
- How are you enhancing your God-given abilities for the glory of God?
- How are you staying aware of opportunities that come your way to enhance God's work?

Accountability is certain and personal (Matt. 25:19). The mature Christian is ready and eager to give an accounting. The mature Christian is prepared for the accounting, knowing that he wants to please the land owner and perhaps reap a reward. The foolish Christian is never ready or prepared but filled with excuses. The foolish servant in this passage failed—not because he was dishonest, but because of his fear. He had received the smallest gift. He didn't have to expend much effort for a return. He had a false understanding of the character of the master. He saw the master as hard, covetous, unreasonable, and impossible to please.

If he had known the Master better, perhaps the outcome would have been different. All had the opportunity for reward, approval, and greater opportunities. But the foolish servant lost his opportunity. It is not what you have; it is what you do with it. We have a great opportunity in our church to change the world; to change business and politics and race relations and to alleviate poverty. Our stewardship consists of attitudes and actions. Our Lord is one of trust, confidence, and love. By applying our best efforts to our best abilities at every God-given opportunity, we are faithful servants. May it be so.

OPPORTUNITIES FOR DAILY LIVING

Question: If you had 100 sheep, would you give the Lord 50? Answer: Of course!
Question: If you had 100 cows, would you give the Lord 50? Answer: Of course!
Question: If you had 100 horses, would you give the Lord 50? Answer: Of course!
Question: If you had only two pigs, would you give the Lord one? Answer: No, I'm afraid not!
Question: Why not? Answer: You know I have only two pigs, so that is not a fair question!

- What is the Lord asking of you?
- How will the Lord judge your giving?
- What talents do you have?
- As the Lord has distributed talents to you, are you holding five, two, or one?

I think the Lord has given to all of us many more talents than any of these. We are not the owners of these talents. We are to invest our talents for the glory of God. God is a fair owner; God expects us to invest a tithe in the expanding of his work.

- How are you using your talents?
- How will the Lord judge your investments upon his return?
- What is holding you back from investing your talents for the glory of God?
- How does fear of your social status, wealth, or false sense of self hold you back?
- How can you move beyond what is holding you back to become a faithful servant?

PRAYER

Lord, find me faithful. Help me overcome fear, selfishness, and my false sense of self. Help me to trust you more, to live into the fulness of my effort. Lord, find me faithful. Amen.

Baptist by choice*

Did you ever stop to think just what it means to be a Baptist and how much it has cost those who have gone before us? Some have thought that the name "Baptist" is merely a label, like "Carnation" on a can of milk or "Ivory" on a bar of soap. But it is not so!

The name Baptist is backed by the Bible and is bathed in the blood of martyrs who loved truth more than they loved their own lives. Even in the early days of our country the three state-established religious groups—Congregationalists, Presbyterians, and Episcopalians—persecuted the Baptists. Sometimes Baptists were even banished from their land to endure more danger. Early American history is filled with man's brutality to man, with even Christian people being inhumane to other Christians. The persecution of Baptists was so great that the great American patriot Patrick Henry, himself a member of the Church of England, provided free legal defense for them.

It was because of Patrick Henry and James Madison and others that Baptists finally won religious liberty. This victory was not just for themselves, but for all expressions of religion in our county. It is a matter of the congressional record that this freedom was begun by and for Baptists. It has also been a matter of tradition that Baptists have stood for complete liberty of all religions.

After we look at what it means to be a Baptist, then you can make up your own mind whether you want to be a Baptist, remain a Baptist, clarify your "baptistness," or become something else altogether.

A Baptist is first a born-again believer. You are not born a Baptist. You may be born into a Baptist family, but you are not born a believer. Each Easter some faith groups baptize babies whose families are told they are being born into the Kingdom of God. Some are crying, some sleeping, some giggling. But none of them are aware of what is taking place. The aim of a parent in dedicating a child to God is understood, but the Bible does not teach that you become a citizen of the Kingdom of God through this process.

John 3:3 says, "Except a man be born again, he cannot see the Kingdom of God." This is the spiritual birth that Jesus explained to Nicodemus. Man must realize his sinful condition and trust that God in Jesus will transform him into this new nature.

In Act 8:36-37 the Ethiopian asked, "What doth hinder me to be baptized?" Philip answered him, "If thou believest with all thine heart, thou may be baptized." Only born-again believers are Baptists.

While some would originally call Baptists "Anabaptists" or "Re-baptizers," the Scriptures would eventually be illuminated and people would discover that personal faith preceding baptism would define Baptists.

Baptists believe completely in the authority of the Bible. For Baptists, the Bible is the trustworthy authority for faith. Some people accept their church as their authority. Some people accept a person as their authority. Some people accept individual conscience as authority. Baptists, however, give total authority to the inspired and true Word of God.

First Timothy 3:16-17 gives us this instruction: "All Scripture is given by inspiration of God and is profitable for doctrine, for reproof, for correction, for instruction in righteousness that the man of God may be perfect, thoroughly furnished unto all good works."

The Bible is not an object of worship, but rather a message from the one we worship. The Bible is to be read with as much interest and affection as any other message from a loved one. The Bible shows us what God is like, what men are like, why we were created, and how to please God. The Bible is a record of the work of God in the world, but the Bible is *not* God!

The Bible is God's Word. The Bible is true and trustworthy. The Bible gives us authority for living all the days of our lives. And the Bible promises that if we claim Jesus as our Lord and Savior, we will spend all the days of our lives in eternity with Jesus and God. I believe that and I claim that for my faith.

Baptists also believe in the personal priesthood of every believer. In the Old Testament only the sons of Aaron were priests. They were born priests. The high honor of being a priest could not be bought, earned, or bestowed as a reward. Priests were born.

In the New Testament the only priests are those who are born again and received into the family of God. This means that all believers are priests unto themselves. You and I have the ability to read and pray and offer worship whenever and however we wish. We give authority to God, who leads us and teaches us. We give authority to the Bible, which teaches us and helps us grow as priests. But the Bible is clear, "Jesus hath made us kings and priests unto God, his father" (Rev. 1:6). I am a Baptist because of all of these things and more.

PRAYER

Thank you, O God, for the continued freedom you give us through your Bible and your grace. Thank you, O God, for the ongoing revelation that guides us to be your witnesses in the world. Thank you most of all for Jesus, who saves us and gives our lives meaning. Amen.

*Eula Mae's lesson files contained several drafts related to Baptist principles. It appears that she shared these ideas not only with her Sunday School class, but also with other groups. While her notes probably date back to the mid-1950s, the final draft appears to have been written much later as the struggle and ensuing division of the Southern Baptist Convention were beginning. Although the Baugh family was deeply involved in trying to prevent this splintering, the "split" eventually occurred. However, new organizations have faithfully taken up the cause deeply embedded in who Eula Mae and John were as Baptists. The Baugh family has been instrumental in helping to carry out the work of the Cooperative Baptist Fellowship, formed in 1991, and of other cooperating groups. A network of partnerships has coalesced around being "free and faithful" Baptists because of the support of the John and Eula Mae Baugh Foundation and the work of thousands of other Baptists. We have chosen to present this lesson and the succeeding one in the language of Eula Mae, who honored other faith groups but was first and foremost a Baptist!

Sharing and observing

Today we continue our discussion of the main "ingredients" of what it means to be a Baptist. The Greek word for church, *ecclesia*, is literally translated "called out." This originally designated an assembly of people called out of their homes and gathered for a reason. For many, the church is also thought of as an institution. But more often, in Scripture the church is spoken of as individual communities, each independent of one another and all working together to share the gospel of Jesus in the world. Baptists have done this in a powerful way throughout the years. And, that takes us to the first Baptist principle of the day: observing the Great Commission.

No one has done cooperative missions better than Baptists. The Southern Baptist Convention established a network of missionaries around the world to share Jesus with the lost of the world. Matthew 28:19-20 gives us our marching orders: "Go you into all the world and preach the gospel, baptizing them in the name of the Father, Son, and Holy Spirit, teaching them to observe all things that I have commanded you." And, we believe that it is the goal of every Baptist to prepare himself sufficiently with the saving truth of God's Word so that he can present the gospel, lead others to Jesus, and disciple believers to grow spiritually deeper.

Some people call this evangelism, some call it discipleship, and some call it witnessing. Baptists have made this all part of our missionary effort into the world. It is following our Lord's command, that we know Jesus personally, that we know his word in order to share it with others, and that we are then able to use God's word to make disciples who will also be on mission with us. I believe strongly in this principle. That's why I teach so strongly that each of us are to be missionaries, using our gifts and sharing our love of Jesus with a lost world.

Baptism by immersion is key to being a Baptist. For more than 200 years Christians have followed the command of the Lord by immersing ourselves in the waters of baptism. Other faith groups practice pouring and sprinkling, some even using just a drop of water. The Roman Catholic Church declared immersion a heresy in the 1300s. But we believe that Jesus was immersed, and we follow what we think was his practice.

Romans 6:4 tells us, "Therefore, we are buried with him by baptism into death; that like as Christ was raised up from the dead by the glory of the Father, even so, we also should be raised to walk in the newness of life." And so we believe that "dunking" is the form of baptism that best depicts the death, burial, and resurrection of Jesus as portrayed in Scripture. There has probably been no disagreement among faith groups that has caused more hurt than the disagreements over the form and purpose of baptism.

Baptism by immersion is definitely not a sacrament, meaning necessary to salvation. Baptism does not save us. Baptism is not required for salvation. If you believe in your heart and confess with your mouth that Jesus Christ is the Lord of your life, salvation occurs. However, baptism does very definitely represent an obedience to identify with a certain community of believers. Being a Baptist means following my Lord's example and command by going down into the waters of baptism.

The Lord's Supper is another ordinance that, like baptism by immersion, sets us apart from other faith groups. As Baptists, we believe in Luke 22:19-20. "When in instituting the Lord's

Supper, Jesus broke the bread saying, 'This do in remembrance of me.'" There is no salvation in participating in the Lord's Supper.

As Baptists, we believe that the bread is not the actual body of Christ. Jesus the Christ cannot be made in the bakery. The cup of the new covenant is not actually the blood of Christ. The bread and the juice are both symbols, used by every saved and believing obedient church member to remember the Lord's death and resurrection until the Lord's return.

The Supper is practiced in loving obedience. As Paul instructed in 1 Corinthians 11:28, "Examine yourselves and only then eat and drink." We observe it regularly, obediently and thoughtfully, remembering the sinfulness of our lives and accepting the grace and blessing of God's forgiveness through the sacrifice of his son on the cross. There is no more moving practice in the Baptist tradition than coming to the Lord's table, remembering Jesus' love for us.

The Cooperative Program—doing work together. Baptists are individual church groups. We don't have a pope or a global leader who commands us to do our work. We are united under the Lordship of Jesus Christ.

Baptists have always pledged our unity to Jesus in a way that has joined us together all around the world. Because we are united in Jesus, we want every lost person in the world to know of his love and grace. Because we are united in Jesus, we share of our resources to larger "clearing house" organizations that build relationships and develop work opportunities to help us share the saving message of Jesus.

In the Southern Baptist Convention there are mission boards that help us do missionary work. There are other groups such as the Baptist World Alliance that help us do missionary work with other Baptist groups around the world. Hundreds of Baptist groups around the world cooperatively share of their resources because we strongly believe that we can do more together than we can do by ourselves.

Some say this cooperation is our weakness, that we need a designated "Baptist pope" who leads our work. But that is totally against the fierce independence of Baptists. But our "unforced" cooperation is a strength that has grown Baptists into a powerful force for sharing the love of Jesus to lost persons around the world. These and other principles are why I am a Baptist and why I am so fiercely committed to protecting these principles for generations to come.

PRAYER

Thank you for the opportunity to freely live out our faith. Thank you for calling us out to share the gospel, for the waters of baptism, for the Lord's Supper, and for leading us in cooperating together to bring the love of Jesus to our world. Amen.

Thoughts on Faith and Life
The Wit and Wisdom of Eula Mae Baugh

Along the way, Eula Mae spiced up her lessons with humor, wit, and wisdom. She was profound and wise, but never "preachy." Rather, she was folksy and certainly in tune with her class members. She had a deep care and intimacy for her class. Often, the margin notes in her lessons conveyed a personal reference to a class member or church member.

The following sayings and illustrations are ones that Eula Mae seemed most fond of or used in more than one lesson. They are included to give insight into the richness of her thoughts and wisdom about faith and life. The sayings, listed in no particular order and in no particular reference to a Bible passage, are a sample of the many humorous and thought-provoking "one liners" found in her outlines. These bits of wisdom could form a book on their own. Some of the illustrations are hers, and others may belong to someone else—Eula Mae rarely gave the original citation—but they are meaningful and inspirational, poignant and indicative of her personality and faith.

To close Eula Mae's thoughts on faith and life, we have included snippets from a letter she wrote to each member of the U.S. Supreme Court in 1992 and also one of her prayers. The letter is indicative of her staunch support for the separation of church and state—and her lack of fear to speak her mind on this subject. Finally, the prayer is a benediction and a challenge for each of us as we go forward to live our faith the fullest.

- The Christian who prays and worries really only worries.
- Right motives and right priorities will always determine worthy goals and wise values.
- Never settle for second best. God always gives us THE BEST.
- It is never hard for us NOT to do things. The Golden Rule requires that we DO something.
- Life gives back what we pour into it.
- Our faith lifts us up that so we, in turn, might help lift another.
- True love always has a price.
- Reaping is hard work. A laborer is one who works hard. God needs more laborers, not just workers.
- Sometimes we find that WE are the answer to our own prayer request.
- God calls us to concentrate on attainable objectives to achieve victories.
- People of God must not fail in their duty to see that the ministers are equipped with reasonable support so that the ministers do not have to dwell on their physical needs.
- Three things that never come back are a spoken word, a spent arrow, and a lost opportunity.
- Our identity is not what we do, but who we are.
- If you want a real test of your faith, try loving someone that you really don't like and whom you believe really doesn't like you. See what God does.

- Nothing offends us anymore. We have compromised with evil so often that something has to be really awful in order for us to turn away.
- Throwing money at a problem never solved the problem. People have to engage the problem.
- When what we do is more important than who we are, we are in big trouble.
- The cure for divorce is to rekindle the flame of love between a husband and wife. Spending less time on things and more time on each other makes love last.
- Evidence often plays little part in what people choose to believe.
- To live an effective Christian life, we need uninterrupted time with Jesus for renewal.
- All that is necessary for bad things to happen is for good people to do nothing.
- Even as deep breathing strengthens the lungs, so endurance under hardship strengthens the soul.
- If you don't want to fall down, stay on the floor. If you don't want to fail, don't try.
- Society is built upon trust, and trust is built upon the confidence we have in another's integrity. Confidence cannot be forced upon us.
- Money is unimportant. We need it only if we don't die.
- 67 nations are closed to traditional missionary work. 83 percent of our nation is unchurched. We must be eager to share the gospel at every point.
- The easiest thing to give away is another person's money.
- I give because of the joy I get from giving to God. I also give because of the trust I have in where my gifts are going and what my gifts are doing.
- God never asks us to do that which we cannot do.
- I love this line from C.S. Lewis: "A good egg doesn't stay that way. It either turns bad, goes flat, or flies away."
- To be happy, a Christian must simply find expressions of his possessions.
- Stewardship is God using people—translating their attitudes into action.
- Your money is not your stewardship. Giving money is only one part of your giving portfolio.
- Uncle Jasper's relatives were all gathered in his lawyer's office for the reading of his will. It read, "Being of sound mind, I have spent all of my money."
- The Lord does not minimize your slightest service. What may be small in our sight may be great in the Lord's.
- We need spiritual vitality as well as intellectual excellence. What a person does with the possessions God entrusts to him reflects his spiritual vitality or lack of the same.
- Wife to husband: "So our money is tight AGAIN. . . . You never told me when it was LOOSE."
- Good intentions are like a corked perfume bottle: the sweetness is all inside. Only when we uncork it does perfume perform its purpose. Some of us need to be uncorked.
- A favorite Bible verse I quote often: "You are so rich in everything . . . in faith, speech, knowledge, and zeal of every kind, as well as in the loving regard you have for us . . . surely you should show yourselves equally lavish in this generous service" (2 Cor. 8:7, NEB).
- A friend recently told me about his churchgoing participation. "I go to church, I listen to the sermon, I leave my money in the plate, and I get the hell out." Do you think God is pleased with this attitude?
- The Bible teaches that the wicked prosper, not because God is morally indifferent, but because he is redemptively patient. Justice comes—but on God's time.

Thoughts on Faith and Life

- The trouble with most of us is that we prefer a trivial life as opposed to a triumphant life.
- The study of the Bible should do more than develop right views about God, man, and man's duty. The study of the Bible should nurture a right and deep relationship with God.
- Freedom is the opportunity to TAKE responsibility, not to RUN from it. Freedom gives every common person the opportunity to become UNCOMMON.
- It takes courage to embrace freedom.
- All nations are under God. Our power is limited by God's omnipotent hand.
- If I give you a dollar and you give me a dollar, we are neither one better off. But if I give you an idea and you give me an idea, we are both smarter. And if I give you encouragement and you give me encouragement, we are both stronger.
- The Jews thought themselves superior in their world. The Greeks thought themselves superior. Romans thought themselves superior. Americans, Russians, British—all think themselves superior. The world has always been filled with arrogant nationalists. This does NOT mean that we shouldn't be PATRIOTS. We love our country. We should recognize, however, that God uses nations for his higher purposes. The highest form of nationalism is to HONOR God.
- "The difference between a politician and a statesman is that a politician thinks about the next election while the statesman thinks about the next generation" (James Freeman Clarke).
- The church can never assume the role of government in society, and government must never assume the role of the church. Government should provide the means for living a fruitful life. The church should provide the MEANING of living a fruitful life.
- God does not want us to come to church simply because the golf course or the stores are closed.
- American Christians have the greatest freedom in the world. Religious freedom, church freedom, freedom of thought, and freedom from want are granted to each of us.
- A supreme law I try to observe is: Quit frettin' about do's and don't's and grow up. Let love take over—no whining. And love others.
- Our problem is that we try to have fruit without cultivating the trees and the dirt.
- You don't teach a baby to be hungry or thirsty. But we do have to teach a baby the right ways to satisfy these instincts.
- You can't put out a fire in a load of hay with a glass of water. Use more water. If a little love isn't working to make right a relationship, increase the dose of love.
- Always step out in confidence on what you know—not what you don't.
- There is no greater inspiration than to feel that someone believes in you.
- Usually it is the unnamed, ordinary folks who do the most. This is certainly true in the Bible, and I have seen it lived out day after day in my own life.
- There is a constant necessity to be ever ready to witness God's work or to participate in it.
- Curiosity may have killed the cat, but it also led to some wonderful inventions like the light bulb and television. Curiosity wets our appetite for knowledge. It is up to us to act upon it.
- Too often the leadership of God is either mocked or ignored.
- Jesus is more interested in the quality of the life we lead than in the elegance of the things we possess.
- Endurance is more than survival. Endurance is active. Endurance is a matter of faith. Survival is more than just waiting for the inevitable.

- Too many people pretend to be God. Watch out for two things in a would-be leader: He seeks to promote his own version of the truth. He tries to attach men more to himself than to Christ.
- People are never a nuisance. We shouldn't deal with them with one eye on the clock as if we are anxious to be rid of them.
- Time is a gift from God to be used according to God's direction.
- We eat by time, sleep by time, work by time, and play by time. We record our accomplishments in terms of time. In heaven we won't need clocks. Hallelujah.
- Jesus does not demand from us things we do not have.
- Sometimes what we think we need is NOT what we really need at all.
- Anything that lures a man to his own destruction must be done away with.
- Jesus said, "I will give you rest"—not a hammock. To me, that means a refreshing rejuvenation that comes after a good night's sleep.
- God is our creator, not just our arranger.
- We do not have to be perfect before God can do something with us.
- In the genealogy of Jesus, God listed sinful Gentile women. That fact alone is so profound that it should get our attention.
- The happy Christian is an influential Christian.
- Life is not a problem to be solved, but a grand adventure to be experienced.
- What goodness can do to evil is greater than what evil can do to goodness.
- A Christian is useless if he has no positive impact on the world for Christ.
- The light of the candle is most important. A candle without a wick is just wax.
- Whenever we sense worry in our life, let it be a call to prayer.
- Worry is useless, needless, and insulting to God. It is like a rocking chair: keeps you busy, but accomplishes nothing.
- When Jesus told the rich young ruler to go and sell his possessions, he was not telling him to despise his wealth. He was telling him to change his attitude toward it.
- Love is never calculating. Love never thinks how little can I decently give. True love desires to give to the limits.
- When someone calls you great, be aware of who said it.
- The opposite of love is neither hate nor hostility. The opposite of love is indifference and a lack of caring.
- It is easier to rebuke a congregation than a single individual.
- Not everyone who is cast into the furnace can come out without smelling like smoke.
- Truth is sometimes clothed in what looks like failure.
- We develop healthy personalities not by the absence of conflict in our lives, but by the constructive handling of conflict.
- The Pharisees believed in salvation by separation, while Jesus believed in salvation by association.
- It is possible to read Scripture, memorize it, and share an examination of it and still miss its message.
- We sometimes measure ourselves by the wrong people.
- Everyone wants to talk about humility, but no one really seems to want to be humble.
- If John the Baptist were alive today, would you want to be his friend?
- What three things made you happy this past week?

Thoughts on Faith and Life

- When our Christianity costs us something physically, spiritually, emotionally and socially, we are closer than ever in fellowship with Jesus Christ.
- Some days the most meaningful words I hear from John Baugh are, "I value you."
- True religion in the end is not one of argument, but of personal experience.
- If strong-enough emotions are present, a crowd can be stirred up to do almost anything. Many people have acted without any reason or explanation when they've become emotionally excited.
- There are two questions I often ponder . . . no three: How do I reflect God's image? How have I changed God's image? What is my responsibility in acting in God's image?
- Too many of us fear life as much as we fear death. The resurrection of Jesus frees us from all fear.
- "I walked a mile with pleasure, she chatted all the way. / But I was none the wiser, for all she had to say. / I walked a mile with sorrow and not a word said she. / But, oh, the lessons that I learned, when sorrow walked with me" (Robert Browning Hamilton).
- Eventually our choice is not between grief and no grief, but between the pain of grieving creatively and that of grieving destructively.
- We can never prevent the birds of sorrow from flying over our hearts. We can prevent them, however, from building nests in our hair.
- Tears are the price we pay for love. Tears are the sign of love we share.
- The authority of the Bible for ME is not the fact of its verbal inspiration. Biblical authority is in the truths of eternal worth it reveals and to which my soul responds.
- Many think that the television show, *Dallas*, is a new and creative story. Read the Bible: actions from the history of Israel make J. R. Ewing look like a saint.
- Some live to have an institution named for them or to have their name on a building. Others spend their lives in the service of others. The choice is ours.
- We need to have more fun. Who's up for a party besides me?
- Shakespeare rightly called life a drama, but it is also a comedy. Just look around. Some of the funniest people I've ever seen are in my mirror.
- Because we are all on a quest for personal discoveries, we all have something to learn from one another. What are you sharing to help others learn?
- Someone has said an optimist in this life is someone who is not paying attention. This is not the definition of a Christian optimist.
- Both gold and character are forged and purified in the fire, but the goldsmith is never far away while the gold is in the furnace.
- As God told Job, God also tells us, "How can you expect to understand everything in all the workings of my world? Just trust me."
- Today's church has been split in so many directions, often by relatively unimportant things, that we have confused and confounded the public. The world may see us as more contentious than relevant.
- If our churches aren't filled with gladness and joy, people will pass us by. We all are saying "Woe is me." We should be singing "Great is the Lord."
- All of us believe in God, so we must sing—and sing joyfully. And if you can't sing on key, sing a bit quietly.
- Americans are the most inquisitive people in the world. We are always asking, "Why?" And yet, sometimes we have to say, "I believe."

- Unless the sincere study of the Bible makes a difference in my life, I have failed in my study.
- What is seen passes away. What is unseen is eternal. And I would add: Have something to do. Have someone to love. Have something to hope for.
- Richard Webb said: "I only know two things with absolute certainty about life. One day I must die. Today, I am not dead yet. Thus the most important question is, 'What will I do in the interval?'"
- If you live with wolves, you will howl like them.
- Living a self-centered life simply does NOT bring joy.

A struggling medical student fell in love with a beautiful young woman in New Orleans. He was a preacher's kid and one of five children. So, of course, he did not have much money. It took all he had and then some to stay in med school. He found a way to finance a beautiful engagement ring—by selling his blood. He would donate blood as often as advised until he had enough money to buy that ring. That young man was my brother. He taught me a lot about love.

A 12-year-old country boy had never seen the circus. His family was poor and could barely afford their survival. As a reward for being a good boy, his daddy said, "Here's a dollar. Go see the circus."

Early that Saturday morning the boy took his dollar bill and went into town in time for the great spectacle of the circus parade. He worked his way to the front of the crowd and was amazed by the band, the acrobats, the clowns, the exotic animals, the trapeze artists, and especially the elephants. At the end of the parade came the traditional poor hobo-looking clown with floppy pants, droopy eyes, and patched clothes. The little boy rushed to the clown and handed him the dollar bill.

The boy thought he had seen the circus when all he really saw was the parade. This is often the picture of our lives. We miss the big events of real life fulfillment while we are only looking in on the parade.

A very active and concerned lady was dismayed that her church had only a very small children's choir at Christmas. "Someone should do something about this," she exclaimed to her pastor. She soon found that she was the answer to her own prayer concern. Shortly, through her own efforts, there were more than 60 children in three children's choirs that sang praises year-round. Oftentimes what we think should be done by someone else in the church is really our calling.

The young man, obviously still a bit inebriated, was standing before the judge on a charge of drunk driving. "Are you guilty?" inquired the Judge. "I'm not sure, Judge, I haven't heard the evidence yet."

Clarence Jordan founded a group in Americus, Georgia, called Koinonia Farms. It is an ecumenical, multiracial, supportive Christian commune of sorts. When Clarence died, he was put into a plain pine box and placed into a hand-dug gravel hole. Legend shares that as he was lowered into the ground, there was a little girl standing by the grave who thought there should be music. Not knowing exactly what to sing, she began to sing, "Happy birthday to you . . ." She knew what death was really about, especially for her friend Clarence and other believers.

In the ever-changing drama of life, I read the "hymnbook" of the Bible:

When I feel:	Then I Read:
Inadequate and lonely	Psalms 6:16-19, 18:1-13 , 40:17
The need for encouragement	Psalm 37:3-5
Like a failure	Psalm 51:10-12
Under great stress	Psalm 46:1, 10
Depressed	Psalm 42:11
Overflowing joy	Psalm 100:1-5
The warmth of God's nearness	Psalm 139:1-6
That goodness doesn't seem to pay	Psalm 37
Gratitude for special blessings	Psalm 5:10-14
Burdened with guilt	Psalm 31
Fear	Psalm 23:4
That happiness has eluded me	Psalm 1:1-3
A need for help	Psalm 119:34, 66
Assurance of God's watchcare	Psalm 121:8
A desire for leadership	Psalm 139:23-24

I'm not using visual aids, questions, or small group approaches today. Can you believe it? But I did decide to run my lesson by John for his opinion. Very shortly he was sound asleep with deep breathing. This really hurt my feelings, and so I shook him awake.

"How could you fall asleep so quickly when you know how much I have put in this lesson and how much I value your opinion?" I asked him rather sternly.

"Honey, you know I love you and I appreciate you as a gifted teacher. And, honey, I want to remind you that SLEEP is an opinion."

That man . . .

Charlie Brown says to Lucy: "I don't have a single person I can call a friend." Lucy says to Charlie Brown: "You should be like me: I don't care if I have a single friend as long as I am popular."

The doctor serving in an agricultural area was awakened at 4 a.m. by a very loud knocking on the door. He rushed to the door, thinking there was an emergency. "What's the matter, what's the matter?" asked the sleepy doctor. "No problem," responded Tom the milk farmer, "You said you wanted to see me first thing in the morning before breakfast. I gotta' go milk, Doc. So, here I am."

We can concentrate on counting our blessings or we can concentrate on counting our problems. I've found that by counting my blessings, I drive out my negative problems. When we lost our infant son I was in a natural state of grief. Then someone shared with me this poem by James Whitcomb Riley:

> Let me come in where you sit weeping,
> Let me, who have not ANY child to die, weep with you.
> Let me weep with you and for the little one whose love
> I have known nothing of.
>
> Let me be of service, say something between your tears,
> That I would be comforting.
> Because, so sadder than yourself am I,
> Who has no child to die.

I began to count my blessings—a wonderful daughter, a marvelous husband, a comfortable home, a great church, good health—and my Jesus wept with me and brought me comfort: "Eula Mae, Eula Mae, all is right in eternity." Bless the Lord, O my soul.

Dear Justice:

The attached excerpts from the Declaration of Independence seem to reveal we are departing from the original intentions of our forefathers. . . Several decisions made by our Supreme Court in recent years give us great concern. There is a great difference between the separation of church and state and separation of God from countrymen.

Respectfully submitted,
Eula Mae Baugh

God, you never promised it would be easy. Life is too short, and love is eternal. Increase our faith, Lord, so that we can forgive without limits and love eternally. I'm still working on it. Amen.

Our Grandmother

A Tribute by Jackie Baugh Moore and Julie Baugh Cloud

Mama:

Every year you took us shopping and spent the whole day with us (grubby little kids) to make sure we had self-confidence and felt like we fit in by letting us pick out outfits that you weren't always crazy about. Now that we look back, we realize that you had so much going on in your own life that we don't know how you did this . . . but you did, and you even enjoyed it.

Many nights we got to pick out a book or two or ten, and you would sit in our bed and read to us . . . the same stories . . . over and over . . . happily and with such expression. "Rikki tikki tembo no sarembo" . . . and we savored every word and went to sleep contentedly. You never mentioned that you might have been watching a T.V. show or reading a book or relaxing from the day. It never crossed your mind or ours.

In the morning you woke us up by asking what we'd like to have for breakfast. You made eggs, bacon, waffles, grits, cereal, muffins, fruit, and more. It all came out at the same time, and we all ate together. It never occurred to us how hard and time-consuming and messy that was. It never occurred to you, either, because you seemed so happy to do it and for us all to eat together.

You always had the name "Dottie Do Good" because you took care of everybody. Any friend or acquaintance who was in need of help, food, or time could always turn to you. You must have been doing for others every day of your life.

Although you might have wanted to go to the movies, have a night out, or just read a book, you never mentioned it; you were too busy thinking of us.

You came to see us play volleyball, cheerlead, play softball, and sing. Although it was cool to act as though we didn't want any parents around, we always looked to make sure you were there. We know you had lots of other things going on in your life . . . you never mentioned the fact that you were a bit busy helping entertain a board of directors, planning a party, seeing people in the hospital, etc. . . . We just knew you wanted to see us.

You sent cards to Sunday School members, studied diligently for teaching lessons, and ran a large department very well. You never tooted your own horn, but yours were always the most well-attended, insightful classes where people knew that someone knew and cared about them.

You put thousands of miles on your car hauling us all over town to activities, always with a smile . . . always with a great deal of patience and diplomacy.

We hope you realize your impact on our lives. You were a role model to so many . . . especially us. Although we are not likely ever be able to do as many things at once, as organized, and as well as you always did, it will forever be a goal for us. You were our family "dream maker" because you made all of our hopes and dreams attainable. Your work with Papo enabled him to be successful, and he was smart enough to realize that although he was visible, you were the control center for our family—the wind beneath our wings, as the song says. We are so grateful.

It is clear that if King David (actually, our Bible says these are the sayings of King Lemual of Massa, but who's picky) had only known you, the Proverbs 31 woman would have been rewritten to go something like this:

If you can find a truly good wife, she is worth more than precious gems (but if you find her, be sure to give her many precious gems).

Papo trusts her with his life, and she has made him a totally contented, fulfilled man. She never hesitates to help him because of her total devotion.

She makes many a prom dress, Halloween costume, fixes hems, buttons, socks, and all critical pieces of clothing that must be done in 20 minutes or the wearer will absolutely die.

She buys imported foods but fixes 14 different dinners so that each family member or guest will be completely satisfied, and they will all eat together happily with her, and she will look like she just stepped out of Glamour Magazine *for the occasion—even though she has been cooking all day.*

She gets up before dawn to have her coffee so that she can prepare a gourmet breakfast for her household and anyone else who stops by.

She plans the day's work and organizes the family's day so that they can all be where they need to be when they need to be—and she can be all places, too. She also works in a hospital visiting and making food for a grieving family.

She inspects a ranch, buys it, and makes it into a home.

With her own hands she remodels a greenhouse to become a playhouse for her granddaughters so they can enjoy every minute of their day.

She is energetic (understatement), a hard worker (cleans the light fixtures at the church in her spare time), and watches for bargains. She works far into the night, looking like a million bucks at a dinner for people she has never met but has discovered their interests so she can entertain the spouses and discuss things important to them.

She seeks the poor so as to generously give of her time and money to make life happy for those God sends her way.

Winter does not worry her because she gives duck blankets to her kids and prepares warm houses and gives them new coats and clothes.

She does look darn good in purple linen but doesn't have time to iron, so her own beautiful clothes are drip-dry easy travel. . . Of course, with her figure it really doesn't matter what she wears: she will turn heads in towns all over the world, and she won't even realize how gorgeous she is—which, or course, makes her even more gorgeous. . . . Her husband is envied by many.

Her husband is well known and sits in the council chamber (or stands so others can have the chairs) but prefers her company because she has cultivated interests that are of interest to him so that their lives are exciting and fun . . . baseball, golf, and other such activities.

She is a woman of strength and dignity and has no fear of age because it can't find her.

When she speaks, countless people of all ages in her Sunday School classes and at Sysco functions are enamored with her wisdom and knowledge: they can't believe that someone with that knockout body and beauty could be that smart, too.

Kindness is truly the rule for everything she says.

To say she is never lazy is quite the truth; we wish she would be at times.

Her children stand in amazement and bless her, and so does her husband because she has been the one who takes care of the whole family and bonds us all together.

There are many fine women in the world but you, Mama, are without question, the BEST of them all!

Charm can be deceptive, and beauty isn't supposed to last, but you changed that rule. A woman who lives her life fulfilling God's greatest commandments of loving him and others shall be greatly praised. These good deeds of hers shall bring her honor and recognition from leaders all over the world, and especially from her family who knows how blessed and honored we are to have her!

www.ingramcontent.com/pod-product-compliance
Lightning Source LLC
Chambersburg PA
CBHW071005160426
43193CB00012B/1928